POSTMODERNIST APPROACH TO Anita Desai

A Socio-Cultural Study of Her Novels

POSTMODERNIST APPROACH TO Anita Desai

A Socio-Cultural Study of Her Novels

Sujatha Rao

Prestige

an international publishing house

Published by
Prestige Books
New Delhi 110 058
Ph. 9818755529
email: prestigebooks@gmail.com
website: asiabookclub.com
ISBN: 81-7851-067-7

Printed at Chaman Offset Press, New Delhi 110 002

Contents

This book is dedicated to my Guruji
Sri Sri Sri Hanumat Kali Vara Prasada Babuji and
Sri Sri Sri Yogini Chandra Kali Prasada Mataj

Preface

Anita Desai is considered the forerunner of contemporary Indian English women's fiction. Women's fiction that has appeared recently all over the world shows certain defiance against the set norms of writing, particularly so, in its depiction of the female psyche. Anita Desai, as a literary artist, is preoccupied with women and the problems they face in a society, which has always been hostile to them. She explores feminist concerns in Indian literature, in a genre she handles so effectively and tries to establish certain norms that oppose the cultural canons. Her characters are the product of new socio-cultural environment ushered in after the collapse of modernism with its emphasis on a literary text as "autonomous." In fact, the entire gamut of women's writings, exploring several issues such as history, sociology, psychology, is an obvious deviation from the modernist elitist art and relates itself to a new phase of history called postmodernism.

Anita Desai, an Indian woman writer, settled down abroad, evokes the postmodernist spirit with overwhelming sense of admiration. Her novels like *Cry the Peacock* and *Voices in the City* have added a new dimension to the genre, in the sense that her books lay open the minds and personalities of the female protagonists exposing the unjust conventions that make women passive slaves to the society. Her novels explore the turbulent psyche of the modern Indian women, their place among the expatriates and immigrants and their personal relationship with men. Anita Desai constantly writes about the irreconcilability between the inner and outer world. The stories she writes are those of ordinary people who are depicted in an extraordinary manner, so that the world of common men and women is marked with literary aura.

Much has been written on the novels of Anita Desai. This book is different from the rest in the sense that it attempts to locate the novelist's concerns during the postmodernist socio-cultural conditions. The book tries to understand postmodernism as a new phase of history with its profound impact upon the creative minds of the people and its relevance to the Indian English women's fiction. The theme is worked out through the following chapters:

Chapter One offers information on postmodernism as the contemporary phase of history. It compares the contemporary socio-cultural conditions with those that produce modernism and endeavours to juxtapose the two concepts within the context of life and literature. The chapter shows the development of new literary concepts, which grows out of the modernist era. It also projects the contemporary social reality and its impact it produced on the creative minds of the people, particularly on the literary artist. The chapter also offers socio-cultural background to the main book.

Chapter Two is about a short historical survey of Indian English fiction. This survey is necessary because it shows the emergence of a variety of trends and tendencies in Indian English novel till it became a genre predominantly handled by women. The chapter also examines the contribution of women writers to the contemporary Indian English novel. Finally, it traces the position Anita Desai occupies among the women writers writing in Indian English.

Chapter Three offers the thematic analysis of the novels of Anita Desai with particular emphasis on socio-cultural and economic background. It is an examination of Desai's novels from the literary point of view relating the content of the novels with the main book. Such novels as *Cry the Peacock* and *Fire on the Mountain* are taken up one by one and analyzed bringing out their relevance to the contemporary phase of history called modernism.

Chapter Four focuses on the postmodernist elements in the novels of Anita Desai. The various socio-cultural issues as against those that deal at the beginning of the 20th century are taken up for study and examined in the light of postmodernist literary concepts. Anita Desai's pre-occupation as a literary critic has always been the exploration of the female psyche. The chapter attempts to relate this exploration from a postmodernist stand as against the modernist reluctance to relate itself with anything that is not literary. Such postmodernist factors are worked in detail drawing them from the novels of Anita Desai.

Chapter Five deals with Anita Desai's technical devices of fictional writing. This chapter concentrates on the modes of narration and the narrative techniques that are practised by the novelist. Desai's narrative is not innovative, but its simplicity, which covers the entire human personality, is amazing. The chapter attempts to relate Desai's narrative techniques with its postmodernist modes of experience.

Chapter Six is the concluding chapter that highlights the conclusion arrived at after a thorough study of Anita Desai's novels in the light of the argument of the book. It offers a brief survey of the preceding chapters and reaches out to the arguments stating the contention of the book. The conclusions are stated pointedly so that the research arrives at a well-wrought end.

I cannot close these prefatory remarks without acknowledging my gratitude to those who contributed to the preparation of the present project. I would like to express my profound gratitude to Professor R.J. Bhongle, Department of English, University of Mumbai, for his encouragement and support and patience in guiding me on the subject. This book would not have come to a fruitful completion without the Divine Grace and Blessings of Sri Babuji and Sri Mataji and my Parents.

I would be failing in my duty if I do not acknowledge my husband and my children Medha and Govind who gave me unconditional love and support while writing this book.

Last but not the least, I would like to thank Prestige Books for the meticulous editing and elegant form conforming to international standards of production.

SUJATHA RAO

Chapter I

Postmodernism: A Contemporary Social Reality

Post-modernism is a contemporary phase of history which encompasses within it range a variety of issues and problems. It is a reaction against the modernist concept of life and literature. Therefore it is necessary to open a discourse on postmodernism with reference to the value and identity of the term "modernism." Modernism is a curious term that recedes into the past as we move forward to postmodernism, postcolonialism, etc. In short, it is a change from the past. It searches for new forms of expression by subversion or rejection of conventional ideologies that have been dominated by cultural and social forces of the previous century. Modernism had a wide influence on life and literature at the close of the 19th century and the beginning of the 20th century. It had cast significant impact on all creative arts especially on poetry, fiction, drama, painting, music and architecture. Some theorists suggest that modernism was at its peak in the 1920s while some others consider it as a new and dynamic movement that petered out by 1940s.

The modernist tendencies were transcontinental and appeared in several European countries like France, Russia, Germany and England, and in America, between the 1890s and 1930s. In India, the modernist tendencies did not appear till 1940s and 1950s when, in fact, the waves of modernism in the West had already abated. The Indian modernist writers aimed at creating protagonists who were quintessential seekers of self-fulfillment and self-realization. The purpose of literature was to capture the individuals' plight in formal, evocative expression, and the mental forces of "time" and "fate." A new style of writing was to emerge which was to be distinctly Indian, without being snobbish or false. The Indian writers have grown to look at the world as part of them, to express the truth of the inner and outer selves. In other words, the works of the writers forged ties in the present with the past and by its cultural spirit translated its ideas, aesthetically and through metaphoric expressions. This was found more distinctly in regional literature than perhaps in literature written in English.

The Dictionary of Modern Thought[1] (Bullock 515) defines modernism as a break from the established rules, traditions and conventions to insist a fresh way of looking at man's position and function in the universe. It is remarkable, in that, it experiments with new forms and styles in writing. Modernism is particularly concerned with language and with linguistic experimentation which brought forth innovative modes of expression. The obsession with experimentation and innovative styles in literature made it unpopular with the new generation of writers which was the product of new socio-cultural milieu. By 1960s modernism came to be considered as a concept for the elite and the arrival of postmodernism was confirmed. The post-world war scenario witnessed several changes. The spread of education and democratic values produced "new culture" asserted by the less privileged classes in society including women. The scientific and technological advancements made life easier. Electronic devices like Radio, Television etc., and the illustrated magazines and newspapers helped the new culture spread wider still. The Civil Rights movement in America, the Feminist movement all over the world coincided with the disintegration of the British Empire. The newly liberated Asian and African countries found place in world organizations like the League of Nations, the UNO etc. World War II was, in fact, a nightmarish experience to those who witnessed it from close quarters; it nevertheless produced some good results as well. The war enhanced the process of women's liberation as women were compelled to come out of the four walls of their houses and earn livelihood, because they had lost their men in the war. The war also enhanced the process of social integration as men from all classes came together and fought against the common enemy—Nazism. The post-World War era was a better age to live in where all classes of society could breathe freely and where the early discriminatory norms in life and literature dropped down on their own. This inaugurated a new era, a new phase of history—now known as postmodernism.

Postmodernism offers a special scope to women in social as well as in literary spheres. Feminist literary movement defies old conventions of writing and encourages women writers to speak freely of the "endless female hungers." (Kamala Das, *The Looking Glass*) The writers also adopt new modes of expression rejecting the canons. The present book concentrates on Anita Desai's writing as an outcome of trends and tendencies that were essentially the outcomes of the postmodernist condition.

The Western socio-cultural trends do not necessarily reflect the Indian condition. While in the West modernism is a matter of past; in India it continues to show off occasionally. One of the connotations of the term "modern" is to awaken to new reality—to face enlightenment. The Indian masses, as indeed the masses in all the Third-world countries, have started awakening to new realities only recently. And, at the same time, they are the product of postmodern condition. Indian leaders like Gandhi, Nehru and Ambedkar, being modernized through Western education, tried to inculcate a new sense of reality among the masses, and their efforts came off considerably. This might not have produced material results as yet; the process of producing such results, nevertheless, can be located everywhere.

Postmodernism is often charged of being a product of capitalist tendencies in view of the fact that it is associated with the new economic policies like liberalization, globalization etc. This, however, is an isolated way of looking at it. The scope it produced for the "have-nots" of the world, for the perpetually exploited sections of the society, the Blacks, the Dalits in India, the aborigines and women are in a position to contribute to the overall development and reap benefits for themselves.

The feminist assertions in every walk of life today are an evidence of the postmodernist scenario in countries like India. Though the miserable plight of the Indian women continues to haunt, a bright future for them can be carved out with determined efforts. The possibility is well within reach. Contemporary Indian literature contains voices of women writers who show considerable concern for the common cause of women. Anita Desai, for example, delves deep into the feminine psyche and displays the sufferings of women caused by tradition.

Internationally, postmodernism is a form of photographic discourse that is constructed upon appropriate images drawn from popular culture. It is broadly outlined as contemporary culture. Jürgon Habermas,[2] one of the most influential proponents of postmodernism, considers postmodernism as "offshoot of Romanticism"; it runs counter to the ideas of Age of Enlightenment. Verily postmodernism is a condition of self-deception of an individual i.e., when critical and rational traditions are devalued and consequently the social structures are pushed towards totalitarianism.

Today, postmodernism is identified with the emergence of the world as a global village. It is a consequence of postmodernist ideas. One position states that 'postmodernity' is a condition or state of being and is concerned with changes to institutions, media and its conditions.[3] Postmodernist thinkers opine that postmodernism is an aesthetic, literary, political or social philosophy that consciously responds to postmodern mind. Hence postmodernism becomes a move beyond modernism, marking the end of that elitist notion of life and literature.

One crucial cultural explosion of postmodernism is that the "baby boom generation" which had grown up with postmodernity as a fundamental outcome of society, rebelled against the political, cultural, and educational power structures. A series of protests and acts of rebellion ranging from non-violent and culturally violent acts of terrorism opposing the policies of the previous age was represented by the younger generation. Violence and discrimination were central to this opposition. The Algerian war, the Vietnam War, laws encouraging racial segregation or laws which discriminated women and their access to divorce sparked off the emotions of the suffering masses. Indeed, the era was marked by a visibly upswing use of marijuana, hallucinogens and the emergence of pop style in music and drama. The ubiquity of radio and television made visible changes in the cultural context. Further, the work of Marshall McLuhan's "Media culture" loosened the local and social normative standards.

The increasing power of IT and the eventually high speed internet have led to the dramatic creation of a new economy. The basic point of this changing cultural context was the collapse of Soviet Union and liberalization of China. For a period, this change of social order was described as *The End of History* by Francis Fukuyama. Also the service economics of the consumers produced an intellectual capital and property rights. While service economics emerged as a separate condition of postmodernism, the rise of "participatory culture" of media appliances also prevailed.

Critics of Postmodernism believe that postmodernity either seeks a reform from within or remains as a passing whim in the social organization. Much of the criticism on postmodernity is narrow, conservative and subjective. Postmodernism rejects the subjective view of the world and tries to reach out to the canvas reflecting wider humanity. It is generally accepted as a kind of widespread culture. It is an ongoing debate on contemporary reality. It appears that in the postmodernist context the future is not going to be what it "need to be" as promised by the writers of 1960s and early 1970s. The most widespread expression of the age is that it is a movement towards sincerity. It is a sociocultural, economic, political and philosophic movement aimed to examine the ideal representation of a whole integrated individual and to give it a fictional treatment. Postmodernism is a term used by philosophers, social scientists and critics to refer to aspects of contemporary art, culture, economics and social conditions as a result of the unique features of 20th century. Among these features are included globalization, consumerism, fragmentation of authority and the commodification of knowledge.

One aspect of postmodernism characterized by literary critic Fredric Jameson[4] (Jameson 53) and geographer, David Harvey[5] (Harvey 42) is the mobility of labour and capital. It is their belief that the conditions of postmodernity lead to a new economic order that followed the Second World War. If postmodernity is a state of postmodern mind, it actually precedes acceptance of postmodern thinking. According to David Harvey, in a purely sociological context, postmodernity is an escape from 'Fordism,' a term coined by Aldous Huxley in his book *Brave New World.* Besides being a socio-political and cultural event, Postmodernism is also marked by the changes in science and technology. The invention of TV, radio, camera etc. enhanced the process of cultural decentralization. New machines in the Industries boosted the production of wealth which resulted in economic consumerism. The life, particularly in the West, moved to the point where total negation of old values became possible. The conventional norms of language, culture, man and the universe etc. came to be looked upon as arbitrary because they represented the views of the privileged few. New aesthetics were formulated; new norms were adopted in arts and literature. This was evident in women's writings, in African-American literature, and in Postcolonial literature which became 'new literature in English' at a later stage. The new writer had adopted unconventional strategies, in both theme and narration. The use of language, modes of expression, the technical devices were all new and baffling to the conventional reader. It was the dawn of a new era. Philosophers and cultural critics called it 'postmodern'.

Postmodern, a historical phase that followed the decline of Modernism coincided with the arrival of several ideologies. Women's Liberation Movement dates as back as late 19th century and early decades of 20th century. But Feminism as an ideology consolidated itself when the Modernist elitism was challenged by the socio-political and cultural trends after World War II. This was a period when several factors in arts, culture, science and technology which ultimately became responsible for the arrival of Postmodernism, were gaining ground.

Thus, the two—feminism and Postmodernism—cannot really be disassociated from each other, even though some feminist artists prefer to have independent ideological existence.

Deconstruction of the prevalent socio-cultural norms, perhaps, is the most important aspect of postmodernism. Feminism and Postmodernism are parts of the same general crisis of cultural authority and they derive strength from Deconstruction theories of thinkers like Derrida, Foucault and Lyotard. Postmodernism puts forth arguments and technique that make gesture of dissent and then make value judgment in the absence of authority. It is a form of scepticism about the authority, received wisdom, political and cultural norms. It challenges the foundation of Establishment. Structuralism, which was a parallel movement with Modernism, reasserted the conventional thinking. For example, it declared the sovereignty of language—its supreme authority in the interpretation of every phenomenon in universe. Poststructuralism, through its Deconstructionist declaration, rejected the authoritative norms of Structuralism. Jacques Derrida's rejection of linguistic authority provides the evidence of 'instability of language'. He said that 'signs' are not predictable entities and there is no 'conjunction' between the 'signified' and the 'signifier'. According to Derrida, words always contain echoes and traces of other words and there is always a possibility of a different meaning of the same 'sign'—and he called it "differance"—a neologism derived from the conventional 'difference' (Derrida, *Structure, Sign and Play in the Discourse of the Human Sciences*). He further contends that all Western Philosophy is based on the assumption that full meaning of a word is present in the mind of the speaker which can be communicated to the listener. He disagreed with this and called it a lie. This was a severe blow to the superiority of the canonical use of language which allowed linguistic flexibility in arts and literature. Conventional thinkers described this as 'crisis of language'.

Michael Foucault is another thinker who turned against the system-building tendencies of Structuralist thought. In Foucault's case, there is a particular interest in the marginalized group who are always excluded from power—such as the insane, the prisoners, the homosexuals etc. The entire Western culture after the Renaissance has been unjust to these groups and has set different norms of behaviour for them. Foucault turns the ancient culture of Greece and Rome and demonstrates that all these societies were tolerant of sexual differences. They accepted both homosexuality and heterosexuality. But the modern civilization discriminates among these groups. (*The History of Sexuality*, 1976)

Foucault's views rejected heterosexuality as norm and authority and approved of different sexual practices like lesbianism. It was another blow to the socio-cultural canons preached and practised in the 'civilized society'. It paved the way for women's liberation from the shackles of social institutions.

The Postmodern condition: A Report of Knowledge (1979) by Jean Francois Lyotard remains to this day the most illustrated example of postmodern theory. Lyotard admits that 'Knowledge is power' but this power is accumulated in the hands of the few who are supporters of 'grand narratives' and who alternately, are the Authority. He therefore proposes that Knowledge should be disseminated and decentralized. He insists particularly on scientific knowledge which controls the world today. Lyotard's objective is to demolish the authority wielded by the "grand narrative" which is repressive of individual creativity. Postmodernism, thus, asserts disbelief in the prevailing ideology which has ceased to have authority to enforce its will.

Postmodernism, however, is not a negative assertion. It endeavours to create and construct value judgment that is acceptable to all. In his book, *Just Gaming* (1979) Lyotard argues that in the absence of any guidance from grand narratives little narrative *(petit recit)* will have to be created which would support the individual and would be his/her guiding principle through the contemporary chaos of beliefs and disbeliefs .

Jean Baudrillard's assumption that the system cannot necessarily be opposed, but it can certainly be "seduced" *(Seduction*, 1979) was yet another challenge to the canonical socio-cultural norms. Most of the major postmodernist thinkers expressed their dissatisfaction with the authority in socio-cultural matters because the authority was oppressive to the individual creativity. It was precisely this argument which the feminist thinkers carried out further and exercised their freedom in arts and literature. This has invariably been a source of inspiration to many women writers writing today. This book presents a detailed investigation and analysis of postmodernism as contemporary social reality with particular reference to Anita Desai's novel.

Literature obeys certain rules and these rules could be systematized. Literary language figures men and women in systematic patterns. With the founding of the National Organization of Women in America, the British Women's Liberation Movement and the Student Revolts in 1968 in Paris, there have been profound shifts in conception of women writers, contemporary culture and subjectivity.

While language is an act of construction, literature holds a mirror to truth. Any literary identity emerges from a shared set of concerns. Beginning from the 1960s there have been radical concerns in humanism, structuralism and feminism. Subjectivity which is a shared technique of postmodernist feminist writers showed women's situation either as the absence of women or as women being marginalized. While the position of women called for a serious questioning, the impact of feminism raised an issue in the postmodern representation of women in the so-called Third World countries. This attitude to women in contemporary India has its roots in tradition. Abroad, the psychoanalytic theories of

Kristeva, Irigaray, Helen Cixous and other prominent poststructuralists offered a good deal of criticism towards an even handed process to women's condition. To subvert the conventions and presuppositions on women, the poststructuralists began to create special space for women. Their rejection of old values helped women carve out a world of their own in contemporary society. Jacques Derrida, the French philosopher and the postmodernist author who coined the term "Deconstruction," influenced American as well as French feminists like Barbara Johnson, Julia Kristeva, Lucy Irigaray, Gayatri Spivak etc. To a large extent deconstruction influenced the feminists in their use of metaphors for gender, ideological patterns, aesthetic forms and literary representations.

Anita Desai's use of metaphors, patterns and aesthetic forms assert the fluidity of women in her novels. This is in sharp contrast to the other writers in whom there is displacement of meaning by redundant figures of speech. According to Gayatri Spivak, deconstruction is useful to feminism technically and more specifically when it is "subject centred."[6] This is evident in Anita Desai's novels which are technically centered and deal with women and their family relationships. Liberal feminism, an influential school of feminist theory, characterizes deconstruction. Thus with the varying strands of poststructuralism, deconstruction, liberal feminism having prepared grounds, postmodernism became an all-embracing contemporary culture. The postmodern situation has inspired a number of creative writers like Chinua Achebe, Wole Soyinka, Salman Rushdie, Anita Desai, Arundhati Roy, who have given the characteristics and comprehensiveness to the concept of postmodernism in literature. These writers through their writings broadened the concept of culture by writing about themes and issues never touched upon earlier.

The novels of Anita Desai seek for a reconciliation of the stylistic disparities of women through writing. Like Sara Suleri, the Pakistani feminist writer, Anita Desai campaigns for "change and new frontiers" of women in India through her novels. This is similar to the campaign advocated by Andreas Huyssen, Leslie Fielder and Irving Home on the international scene.

Postmodern fiction is characterized by a play of genres devaluing high art and realism. This idea is demonstrated by many postmodern writers through their writings. An emphasis on the surface rather than on the structure, represented by the leading postmodernists like Baudrillard, Lyotard and Jameson, seems to be the compelling discussion of postmodernism. Further a constant revision of the surface culture dissolves boundaries between high and low art and creates new artifacts of cultural contexts.

Linda Hutcheon's *A Politics of Postmodernism* (1988) suggests that all institutions of "academic disciplines" artistic conventions and histories make a parody of traditions. Postmodernism is a way in which literary identity asserts itself through parodic and intertextual relation to tradition. Postmodernism's appeal to feminists is due to the fact that women are marginalized by culture. *In the Discourse of Others: Feminists and Postmodernism*, Craig Owens, a postmodern critic, argues that postmodernism would have a real future only if it listened to 'the feminist voice.' The essential feminity which marginalized women throughout history—the divide between the pubic and private—has to be ruptured.

According to Alice Jardine the interest in consumerism and women was frequently utilized by male writers while attacking society. To countermove this notion, Jardine points out in *Gynesis* that "an increase in the writing of theory and fiction by women about women . . . [would] restore women's place in society."[7]

Also, the focus on contemporary women by the Australian critic Meaghan Morris is in a way of Michael Foucault's notion to turn women into consumers and objects of knowledge. Morris argues that 'women enjoy fashion and shopping' in *Things to Do with Shopping Centres.*[8]

It is ironic that postmodern aesthetics have reduced women to shopping animals whose 'pleasure power' and the cultural language are 'double-coded'. Susan Suleiman, argues that postmodernism is controversial not because "of what it is but of what it does."[9]

To enunciate the position of postmodernism is to bring a work of literature close to the reader. There are problems in identifying postmodernism in literary texts, but writers like Gabriel Garcia Marquez, Salman Rushdie and others have demonstrated the postmodern trends in their works. A new sense of history, fragmentation, paranoia, pastiche, juxtaposition of the high and low etc. have emerged as important features of the postmodern writings.

Anita Desai's novels do not necessarily display these features but a sense of belonging to a new era and the possibility of being associated with the rebellious spirit that prevailed after the fall of modernism should place her creative urge close to the postmodernist sensibility. One thing is certain, that she is a product of those socio-cultural factors which opened up into new phase of history now known as postmodernism. Her novels, almost all of them, demonstrate the new socio-cultural trends that set in after the fall of Empire which was a supporting pillar of Modernism.

The 'women-question" today is a global contemporary issue. Anita Desai's preoccupation with women and their problems brought to the forefront the feminist concerns in the Indian subcontinent. The new socio-cultural condition began to offer postmodernist strategies to establish socio-cultural norms and alternate canons to raise the status of women. These were the products of new changing environment. No story could be told without perhaps the socio-cultural aspects. Hence with the collapse of canonical norms in Independent India, the literary text acquired a new autonomy. Art, history, culture, society, psychology began to relate themselves, subverting the conventions, as it were, to this new phase called postmodernism.

The expatriate Indians like Anita Desai evoked an overwhelming sense of the unjust conventions and practices that exploited women in society. The portrayal of startlingly socio-cultural discrimination against the female protagonists stood a contrast to the modern image of India. The new relationship of women with men and other expatriate features marked postmodern culture or became 'novelistic.' So, what emerges is a shared set of the social structures and how it dictates the roles and interactions of the gendered subjectivity. It is the interrogative account of these characters and how they direct themselves to everyday thinking and living is what makes Indian novels a subject of postmodernism.

The novel today narrates the stories of ordinary people whose voices need to be heard. Irreconcilable with the inner self and the outer world, the characters construct social structures, cultural contexts and language codes. While language cannot be isolated, literature becomes an expression of the socio-cultural milieu. While the feminist writers condemn social differences in the postmodernist era, society chooses to marginalize certain social groups and elevate the other. It is a novelist's concern to show them how relationships need to be created and expressed in particular social and cultural contexts to recover the under-represented groups of society. In the postmodernist perspective, the feminist has proved to be literally unavoidable. The ways in which questions on gender, sexuality, reading, writing, subjectivity, enunciation, voice and performance are raised, are unthinkable without the impact of feminism, even though many of these activities occur within the margin or outside.

Anita Desai's works have been researched enormously on the lines of feminist literary criticism, but the representations of women's independence demands a specific exploration as a case study particularly in the light of postmodernist concerns. A new approach to the contemporary social reality has to be experienced by the younger generation. There is a great need to relate these approaches to global trends and tendencies in postmodernist literature. The new learning calls for an exposition of the workings of domestic fiction with a detailed explanation of its conceptual developments.

In a world threatened by nuclear war, we live in a society of language discourse and ideology which do not convey a sense of being and meaning so much. Whatever happens by chance and contingency results in fragmentation or discontinuity. Since there is no coherent explanation of experience, the form of narration becomes superficial and challenges anything that is considered decent. It calls for reconsideration of the marginalized aspects of life and elements of society. The postmodern concept is to integrate art and life and celebrate the 'anti-authoritarian'. The postmodernists write to an audience which is largely disengaged from the activities that the author lives in and as a result their representations seem seamless.

The paradox of postmodern thinkers is the conflict between that latent tradition and emerging doubt. It is different to get out from the weight of a long tradition of visual and narrative representations; and on the other hand, we seem to be losing faith in the existing representations. Indeed it is such implications which make postmodern art paradoxical. However, postmodern and postcolonial are conceptually coherent and in real sense are identical. As a metaphor, postcolonialism creates an urge to read about colonized societies and their cultures. Every postmodernist researcher may not have the historic and linguistic breadth of the movement to get the right impetus. Many postmodern writers write in native languages and translate works into English. Anita Desai is a consummate writer who wrote in English and introduced the psychological novel. She sees India through her father's sentiments. Anita Desai never considered publishing her works in India and strangely it was in England that her work was noticed first. It is with the writing of stories in English that her status of writing on feminist issues drew attention. The feminist movement in India had been a new phenomenon and Anita Desai finds Indians impatient with her books as they think of them as books only about women .They find it somewhat unreal that women don't fight back.[10]

As a writer of both major and minor fiction, Anita Desai is concerned mainly with the workings of the inner self, the tensions between the family members, the reclusive existence of everyday life and the haunting experiences of alienation in middle class families. She is equally preoccupied with German anti-Semitism, westernization of the Indians, the under-privileged pitted against the rich businessmen, the meaningless traditions and other minor aspects of the life that creates rift between the old and the new.

Anita Desai presents the Indian society, Indian politics, Indian socio-cultural milieu through different voices. Postmodernist representations, however aesthetically drawn, may be paradoxically self reflexive. She drifts away from feminism but only occasionally to feel that every stone has a history to tell or largely dwells on the encounter between India and the West. India is always in the foreground of her literary works; she progresses from childhood to marriage, and to motherhood with no break at all through a narrative technique that is always well-wrought. Writing, teaching and sharing family responsibility, Anita Desai is best understood through her works. Her commentary on postmodern Indian women provides coherence and meaning to modern life through the celebration of technological developments. The people she portrays represent the complex, correlated life styles in the postmodern society.

To understand Anita Desai's women, one must comprehend the demons that haunt them, the motivations that shape them, the doubts that plague them—all of which call for a socio-political, economic exploration of her works. Women in Anita Desai's novels offer a fertile ground for study. Not only are these women intense, complex and riddled with seemingly irreconcilable contradictions; they also transform Anita Desai's career into a writer of international repute. A systematic analysis of her novels offers exhaustive information on the postmodernist approach from its debut to the contemporary phase with occasional detours and flashbacks. This help to find an insight into the open-ended dimension of the postmodern movement.

A number of contemporary Indian writers wrote on the themes of family drama, generation gap and divorce. The most significant names among them are: Homen Bargohain, Padma Barkateki, Navakanta Barua and Umakanta Sarma in Assamese; Ashapurna Devi, Pratibha Bose, N. Mitra, Narayana Sanyal, Bimal Mitra in Bengali, Shiv Kumar Joshi in Gujarati etc. But women responded more comprehensively producing very serious fiction, depicting the changing social scene and the change in the sensibility of Indian women. There are many significant men writers who joined this group of women. Some of them are Verma Yashpal, Bendre, U.R Anantamurthy, Bhalchandra Nawade, Mohan Rakesh, O.V. Vijayan and others who followed the socio-political trend set by earlier masters. The greater part of readers consisted of women, not to forget the many female practitioners of the art.

If women's liberation on the global scene had brought with it a whole bandwagon of booties to women to advance their economic and intellectual status, in India, the issues were different. It was not the question who brings the bigger pay packet, or who would do the dish washing, change nappies and wash the curtains etc. If these were the priorities in the West, for the Indian women, the problems were different. It is not just economic equality that she has to fight for. It is social equality and emotional independence that she has to achieve. The problems of the urban working women were no different from the problems of the rural women. In both rural and urban situations, she is the last to be hired and first to be fired. Madhu Trehan and Sunil Sethi explain the situation of Indian woman:

> Her own situation is so inextricably intertwined with her husband's economic condition, that questions such as why she is being paid half of her husband's economic condition, that questions such as why she is being paid half of her husband's salary for the same amount of work on construction site or why she has to manage all the housework alone after working outside all day, become semantic—only to be considered as finer points of living.[11] (Sethi 33)

In such a milieu what is of paramount importance is survival. The Indian woman seeks to be delivered of bondage by love and not by manipulation, regardless of class, caste, religion and community. Though novel is imported basically from the West, the situation of women of any country could be portrayed within the scope it offered. The narrative form of fiction can powerfully depict her biological, psychological, economic, sociological and political condition. Fundamentally, the Indian woman is defined by a set of relationships and modes of conduct within a given society. There is a need here to evolve dialectic of feminism. The existing limitations of the portrayal of all the sections of women are inherent, points out Krishna Ahooja Patel:

> Much of the current writing has tilted more towards examining the position of women in the urban and modernized sector of societies, concentrating on those who are already educated and employed . . . the very real problems of men and women whose backs are bent with hard work in rural areas and whose labour is frequently unrewarded have held the interest of only very few writers.[12]

The woman in India has more dimensions to her plight than the western woman. She has formidable problems confronting her. She has to throw off the shackles of karma, inaction and self-pity to overcome the legacy of centuries-old humiliation, dependence, resignation and silence. The novel in India constitutes a rare region of enlightenment wherein the Indian woman picks up enough courage to raise her head and asks a few awkward but pertinent questions. The responses from readers would determine the shift towards the new development strategies in the Indian social polity. Such has been the influence of traditional portrayal of women. It is this cumulative influence on Indian women in literature and society which makes them essentially committed to rituals, customs, tradition and family. Rama Mehta, a sociologist from Harvard University, aptly describes the changed situation of Indian women.

The social and political reformers like Raja Rammohun Roy and Mahatma Gandhi endeavoured to ameliorate the position of women in India. All discrimination based on sex disappeared with the Independence and the way of life of a whole generation changed radically. Added to this was the cumulative impact of the British influence in education, law, politics and social reform.

The Hindu Code Bill and the Sarada Act have been milestones in the life history of Indian women. Anita Desai, the first postmodern woman writer, brings out the surface realities and the underlying truths about women. Desai makes it explicit in an interview with Yashodhara Dalmia:

> One preoccupation can only be a perpetual search—for meanings, for value, for—dare I say it—truth. I think of the world as an iceberg—the one-tenth visible above the surface of the water is what we call reality, but nine-tenths that are submerged make up the truth and that is what one is trying to explore. Writing is an effort to discover and then to underline, and finally to convey the true significance of things.[13]

Anita Desai makes an attempt to explore this submerged truth through the exploration of the psyche of her characters through her own vision of life wherein interpersonal relations have become absurd. They are hardly able to give emotional or spiritual sustenance, conforming to a sound routine of drudgery. There is no freedom and individuality, all vocations and avocations appear monotonous and senseless. Life is hardly worth living or pursuing. The world is full of violence and destruction and the death threatening every minute, an individual feels lonely and alienated. He is hopeless and full of despair, actually conscious as he is of a sense of the worthlessness and absurdity of all objects and patterns around him. Faith in God that could have provided some sustenance to this hopeless dark world is not sought by Desai's intellectual characters with nothing to lure. Almost all her characters revolt against the existing patterns of life; but as they do not have anything to fight for, their fight remains half-hearted and ends in failure. Sometimes instead of fighting, they tend only to withdraw; but to their shock they realize their attempts are futile because withdrawal is impossible. If they try to seek relief in another world i.e., the world of fantasy, books, social life, subterfuge etc. they come to realize that they cannot escape the reality. They are entangled, trapped with no door to exit.

Life appears meaningless and we are continuously assaulted in our existence that we ought to face life and adapt to make an effort to find some meaning in it. It is from this vision of life that Anita Desai's novels emerge with a cluster of themes whose main ingredients are interpersonal relations, alienation, obsession with death, cruelty and violence, psyche and withdrawal, conformity and non-conformity, which are the deadly clutches of harsh reality and impersonal forces of time and place.

Basically, Desai seems to be saying that the longer one lives, the deeper he/she suffers from the bitter assaults of existence like Nanda Kaul in *Fire on the Mountain.* The change to a more positive attitude like Bim in *Clear Light of Day* is also noticeable. In it, it is love that sees the meaning and perfection of life. In *Custody* the author seems to be advocating a welcome even to the calamities of life. From desperation and depression, the characters mature into courage and positive thinking.

Anita Desai's novels represent the contemporary notion of women's writing. She is a creative artist who approached women's issues from the feminist point of view though she never claimed herself to be one. Thematically, she moves ahead of modernism which did not allow woman to break through the shackles of tradition. Virginia Woolf's essay 'A Room of One's Own' is an expression of an anguished soul acknowledging the necessity of freedom for women. Modernism, in all its vulnerability, was the most imbecile expression of anti-social feelings. The Modernist artist was no visionary, but a cracked mirror which reflected a distorted image of its own self.

The decline of Modernism also facilitated and clarified the concept of centre and periphery. It was now that neglected social classes, including women, started asserting themselves. It was now that women critics in France, Britain and America branched out in the various schools of Feminism. It was now that women writers could write about their own experiences with full confidence and were acknowledged as creative artists.

The conventional authority associated with author, text, custom, social institution, religion, culture, society etc. came to be questioned. Terms like subverting, dismantling, remapping etc. became key phrases in the realm of literary criticism. Overall, it was a phrase for celebration to those who were suppressed and oppressed by the authority and a phase of serious concern for those whose authority was challenged. Historians and cultural critics, considering several factors together described this period as "postmodern."[14]

A woman writer, exercising her freedom to write and rejoicing in her new status, was certainly a product of the Postmodernist condition. A feminist corresponding to various schools of that ideology inevitably subscribes to postmodernism, which includes within its range, every act and effort that subvert conventional thinking. A feminist is also a Postmodernist, at the same time.

It is in this conceptual framework that Anita Desai is being considered in the present study. The following chapters focus mainly upon the socio-cultural aspects of her novels, trying to bring out the features that make her a Postmodernist writer.

NOTES

1. Alan Bullock Oliver, Stally Brass and Stephen Trombley, ed. *The Fontana Dictionary of Modern Thought* (London: Fontana Press, 1990), pp. 515-16.
2. Jürgon Habermas, "Modernity—an incomplete project," *Foster* (1983): pp. 3-15.
3. Anthony Giddens. 'Modernism and Postmodernism,' *New German Critique*, 22, 1981, pp. 15-18.
4. Fredric Jameson. 'Postmodernism, or the cultural logic of late capital', *New Left Review,* 146, 1984, pp. 53-92.
5. David Harvey. *The Condition of Postmodernity: An Enquiry into the Origins of Cultural Change* (Oxford: Blackwell, 1989), p. 42.

6. G. Spivak. 'Feminism and Deconstruction, again: negotiating with unacknowledged masculinism,' in T. Brennan, ed., *Between Feminism and Psychoanalysis* (London: Routledge, 1989), p. 214.
7. Alice Jardine, 'In the name of the modern: feminist questions d'après gynesis,' S. Sheridan, ed., *Grafts* (London: Verso, 1988, p. 15.
8. M. Morris, *Things to do with Shopping Centre*, S. Sheridan, ed., *Grafts* (London: Verso, 1988), p. 4.
9. S. Suleimann, *Subversive Intent: Gender, Politics and the avant-garde* (Cambridge, Mass.: Harvard University Press, 1990), p. 48.
10. Feroza Jussawalla and Reedway Dessenbrook, ed., *Interviews with Writers of the Postcolonial* (Press of Mississippi, 1992), p. 8.
11. Madhu Trehan and Sunil Sethi, "Indian Women—A Time for Reckoning." *India Today* (August, 1.15, 1980), p. 33.
12. Krishna Ahooja Patel, "Another Development for Women" in *Approaches and Strategies*, ed. Marc Nerfin (Uppsala the Dag Hammarskjöld Foundation, 1977), p. 70.
13. Yashodhara Dalmia, "An Interview with Anita Desai," *The Times of India*, Sunday, April 29, 1979, p. 13.
14. Arnold Toynbee, *A Study of History* (Oxford University Press, 1960), p. 4.

Chapter II

Contemporary Indian English Fiction: A Brief Survey

The novel, basically the western genre, has influenced the literatures of all the written languages in the world. This may be due to its facility and accessibility to the average literate and the interest it holds for the common man due to its parallels to life. Many a writer has used this form to represent the real life, which is mostly contemporary to him. If in the past a writer was moved by the issues around and expressed himself in poetry, from the nineteenth century the writers have been mostly using the novel form to express their concerns about human life. In the twentieth century when the stage has been replaced by the movie, and later by the television, the form of drama had been limited to express the social concerns and problems. On the other hand, the novel has grown enormously comprising all the aspects of human life; and, in addition, fiction dealing with suspense like the detective novels and dealing with the fantastic and imaginary worlds like the Harry Potter series, have also become popular.

In recent years, issues concerned with social reality have become the preoccupation of the novelist. This has made a significant genre because it incorporates all aspects of life. The response of the novelist is best described in a novel. It is this response of the novelist that is important to make the experience of the novel real and universal.

The twentieth century India before independence was stirred politically. Efforts were made to overthrow the imperial rule. Liberation became the single motto and the prevailing spirit was an ideological unity. Alongside with this epilogue was the history of English education, which led to the advent of Indian Writing in English. It is a definitive history that integrated cultural, political activism and philosophy for a free and united India. The ideology of Gandhi, his code of morality, tolerance and self-sacrifice prevailed everywhere. As a result of collective efforts, India became free in 1947. Nevertheless, colonization left indelible marks on the Indian psyche. The British were driven out; but the English language remained. Due to the multi-linguistic setting of India, English was continued and it became the major language of expression for the Indian writer. The freedom achieved almost after a thousand years, opened new doors to hitherto unseen arenas and both men and women started expressing eloquently the basic problems that had troubled them since long.

It was the rhetoric of Independence which manifested the Indian writing in English. The creative writers found English not pliable to Indian themes. They had to adopt alternative patterns of writing depicting native themes in a foreign language.

It was then widely realized and accepted that in the ideology of human experience, the female experience must be given a fairly equal importance of expression. History has failed to find adequate expression of the female experience. The freedom struggle under the leadership of Gandhi brought in women from all stratas of society so that it became possible to craft a common platform of free spirit to both men and women after Independence. Thus, the freedom movement of the country played a role not only in the development of political consciousness, but also in literary sensibility.

On the Indian scene, the novel in the native languages started in early 1700s. But Indian Fiction in English could come into existence only after English was introduced in Indian educational system. The early writers and thinkers considered English a language of progress and wrote mostly to effect reforms in the conservative Indians. The imparting of English education started as early as 1717 in Chennai, 1718 in Bombay and 1720 in Calcutta when Raja Rammohun Roy founded Hindu college in Calcutta in 1817 which became a centre of intellectual activities. Later, when East India Company decided to introduce English as a language of educated, it changed the national scenario within a span of 50 years.

The introduction of English in India was prompted by three main objectives—commercial, political and religious. The cultural arrogance of the empire was of course the basis underlying it. It became obvious when Lord Macaulay declared that a single self of European books was worth hundred labourers in India. Charles Grants, Macaulay's colleague and collaborator, made further efforts to implement the education policy which was chiefly meant for consolidating the political grip on the nations, for enhancing the trades and propagating Christianity in India. The sustained efforts on the part of the British produced the desired effects. A large number of 'Brown Sahibs' and 'babus' were ready to help the administration with contempt for the natives. East India Company had successfully adopted 'Divide and Rule' policy.

English education, however, proved to be a boon in disguise. English became a common language of communication among the educated Indians. They could put their minds together and discuss the national issues. English education also brought new ideas into Indian milieu. Unfortunately, Sanskrit education in India remained confined to a particular community which never allowed others to share it. As a result, the lofty notions that lie scattered in ancient Sanskrit texts like the Vedas, the Upanishads, the epics and *Bhagwadgita* never belonged to the nation, but to a caste which took immense pride and pleasure in its superiority in the hierarchy. Nation was never its priority. No wonder, the new language brought in by the colonizers became instrumental in awakening the nation. It was the rise of nationalism on the new horizon.

English education also brought in liberal ideas and scientific vision. Such notions as human dignity, individual freedom and national identity were sown and cropped up in the form of resistance to the Empire. New ideas set in as several young minds relished the new educational atmosphere. Henry Derozio, a celebrated teacher of the Hindu College became a household name; Kesub Chunder Sen a humanist linked India with England. Kashinath Telang and Ranade (called the father of Indian Economics) were intellectuals of modern civilization who shared their aim of life of fullness. With a wide outlook on life and humane sentiment they seized the moment through remarkable and spirited writing. Conjuring up the image of India, Sir Narayan Chandavarkar an orator and politician along with many impressive personalities, tried to modernize the vernacular speech into social instruments of change. It was Ramakrishna Paramahansa who defined the best of the West to India. Vivekananda's writings and speeches were a dominant spirit of essentially educative value. Further, the translation of Western classics became the new literary phenomenon. The English education also opened up a new way to look at the orient resulting into a movement now known as Orientalism. Indology was yet another branch of knowledge that offered a way for the Europeans to know India better. Such books as Tilak's *Artic Home of the Vedas*, Dayanand Saraswati's speeches and writings, several discourses on ancient Indian tradition by the natives as well as the Europeans like Sir Charles Hume, Annie Besant produced towards the end of 19th century, what is now known as the Indian Renaissance, coupled with a general awareness of the national issues.

English also became a language of poetic expression. Several English-educated young men and women, under the impact of English Romanticism, started writing poetry. Henry Derozio was the leading light who showed them the way to the divine gift of poetry. Romanticism became a source of inspiration to young people like Michael Madhusudan Dutt, Ramesh Chandra Dutt, Manmohan Ghosh, Toru Dutt and others. These poets wrote imitative poetry modelled on the works of English Romantics. Most of them are forgotten today, except perhaps Toru Dutt who wrote poems dealing with native themes.

As the twentieth century dawned upon the world, Indian political struggle gained momentum. The whole nation was stirred, as men and women from all stratas of society joined the struggle under the leadership of Gandhi. Creativity in English by the Indians also began to flourish. Tagore, who wrote mostly in Bengali, his mother tongue, translated his own works in English. His collection of devotional poems *Gitanjali* won Nobel Prize in the year 1913. Aurobindo Ghosh, the freedom fighter among the extremist group of young Indians, gave up politics for poetry and meditation, settled down at Pondicherry where he carried out his poetic career combined with meditation. Aurobindo's poetic reputation rests mainly on *Savitri* a long narrative poem based on the myth in the *Mahabharata*, where Savitri a woman of self will and dedication, wins over death that was supposed to take away her husband. Sarojini Naidu has the reputation of being the finest lyrical poet of her time. Praised by Mahatma as the 'nightingale of India' Sarojini Naidu gave up poetry for politics and joined the freedom struggle. She became a staunch supporter of Gandhi and participated in several Satyagrahas led by Gandhi including the famous Dandi March.

Fiction in Indian English at this time also saw better days. Earlier efforts by Bankimchandra Chatterjee who wrote *Rajmohan's wife*, and Krupabai Satyanand's *Saguna* and *Kamala* in English did not receive critical appraisal till recently.

The founding fathers of Indian English novel—R.K. Narayan, Mulk Raj Anand and Raja Rao began their literary career during the early decades of the twentieth century. They set trends which culminated later at the hands of younger novelists like Bhabani Bhattacharya, Manohar Malgonkar, Khushwant Singh and others. R.K. Narayan, Mulk Raj Anand and Raja Rao wrote on different themes and issues, but they caught successfully the ethos of Indian society. Narayan chose to write about the middle-class life in the south, creating an imaginary town called Malgudi where all his major characters are located. Mulk Raj Anand, with his leftist inclination, wrote about the lower classes in such novels as *Untouchable* and *Coolie*, whereas Raja Rao wrote about the Brahmanical tradition and its impact on 20th century life through novels like *The Serpent and the Rope*. Novel became a living literary genre that fused the different narrative forms, and offered a pleasant reading experience. Nirad C. Chaudhuri's work portrayed the Indians' attachment to the river; Narayan's novels centered in *Malgudi* on Sarayu; Mulk Raj Anand's narratives captured the solitary individual and the collective states of minds which had unsavory aspects of life as well as its variegated richness. It was Narayan's novels that were open-ended and creative with the motif of renewal and restoration. Bhabani Bhattacharya's novels mediated on the last years of the British regime to the first years of Congress rule. The ramifications and intricacies of human action remained an unresolved paradox to writers and readers. Manohar Malgonkar's novels exhibited an authentic quality of the clash of the army and civilian code of life. The narrative touches are filled with strange and antique nuances on the shame and glory of partition. The author's note states succinctly in the title *A Bend in the Ganges* (1964) which comes from the *Ramayana*. At a bend in the Ganges, Rama, Sita and Lakshmana paused to take a look at the land they were leaving. (431)

Though it is an attempt to unfold the national tragedy under the guise of fiction, it is a tribute to Manohar Malgonkar's virtuosity. Nevertheless, Bhabani Bhattacharya's *So Many Hungers* (1947), R.K. Narayan's *Waiting for the Mahatma* (1955) and Kamala Markandaya's *Some Inner Fury* (1957) are compelling accounts of the writers' personal experiences of partition. The horrors of partition critique the reality of sensation which challenges the national obsession with borders. The drama of shame and degradation of the Indians and Pakistanis who resented the two-nation theory is best described in Khushwant Singh's *Train to Pakistan*. Kamala Markandaya's personal perspectives on the events of history are explorations on the continuity of history evident in *Some Inner Fury.*

Indian Writing in English moves from the national to the personal; from freedom struggle to gender discriminations to present the different perspectives and happenings. The imposed perspectives deconstruct the knowledge structures legitimized by the imperial discourse. The postcolonial discourse is a search for the hidden layers of meaning, through succinct narratives. The horrors about the partition and the racy details about emergence of writers like Nayantara Sahgal, Salman Rushdie and Rohinton Mistry are landmarks in the political history of India.

The political freedom achieved in 1947 had also brought in changes in the social and personal lives, and consequently, in the Indian writing in English. As women's education was recognized as an important aspect of the free India, the government introduced certain schemes and measures encouraging education for girls. The consciousness that was born and developed in women during the final phase of the independence struggle and the participation of the Indian women in the freedom struggle had also helped in improving the position of women. The inspiration given by the participation in the freedom struggle, and their education later, resulted in producing a group of women writers in India. From then on, both men and women writers concentrated on the themes concerning both the sexes. A number of young writers from different stratas of Indian society began to write fiction in English. Several of them preferred to stay abroad and wrote about the memories of their stay in India. They showed their awareness about the happenings at home and wrote about such political events like Emergency of 1975.

Rohinton Mistry's *A Fine Balance* dwells in great detail upon imposition of Emergency and its repercussions. Allan Sealy's experiment of the 'nama' records the events of history along with the changing power structures of the Trotter family in the book titled *The Trotter Nama.* Amitav Ghosh gives a glimpse of first-hand personal familiarity with the Indian reality. The Indian reality had different meanings of displacement, exiles and migration or Diaspora. Indeed, many Diaspora writers have been pushed to the margins. Though writers like Amit Chaudhari, Sunetra Gupta, Leela Dhingra and Meera Syal are outside India, they did respond to cultural situations and created great critical interest. On the other hand Salman Rushdie's *Midnight's Children* represents the fragmented identities of 'displacement' and 'rootlessness.' Significantly the novel *Midnight's Children* becomes a truly postcolonial account against the backdrop of Indian government. Many women writers such as Githa Hariharan in *The Thousand Faces of Night* and *The Ghosts of Vasu Master* and Nina Sibal in *Yatra* use English without any colonial associations.

The novels of 1980s present the family histories and provide a family tree like Shashi Tharoor's *The Great Indian Novel* and Vikram Seth's *A Suitable Boy* which are crowded with lives and places. Shashi Tharoor's *The Great Indian Novel* and Upamanyu Chatterjee's *English, August* have a touch of rural or small town Indian life. The agony and ecstasy of urban Indian transcends the historical Indian legacy to bring out the postcolonial experience. Given their thematic preoccupation of the individual, Rushdie, Tharoor, Amitav Ghosh, Githa Hariharan and Vikram Chandra moved away from the novels of the preceding decade.

Nayantara Sahgal's novels have a childlike truth which pace into past and present. It is Arundhati Roy, who makes a fine use of the stream-of-consciousness technique so effectively that the novel becomes a chiselled piece of perfection. But, unlike NRI writers such as Raja Rao whose only theme was the India of their memory, novelists like Rushdie and Bharathi Mukherjee show a tendency for a movement towards internationalism. Bharathi Mukherjee's fiction reveals the emotional psychic consequences of the Indian women immigrants.

The determination to explore the ugliness of reality, emotions and the fragility of relationships has resulted in the writing of displacement where writers like Ruth Jhabvala, Kamala Markandaya and Anita Desai disclaimed or distanced from India. Their writings set the tone to the diasporic genre of writing.

The Independence has also influenced the thematic concerns of women novelists. Participation in the Indian freedom struggle leaving cozy and restricted setting of their homes, gave Indian women a taste of freedom in the open air. Women started thinking about the long forgotten Indian ideals of equality and fraternity. While the Vedic India considered men and women as equals and the entire world as one single family, later development in the social structure resulted in the total loss of freedom for women, and confined them to their small homes. This confinement transformed the image of Indian women into a 'Devi' who was worshiped but had no say in the household or political matters of the nation. Centuries of this confinement of Indian women affected the mind of the Indian male too. The balance in the Indian society vanished and created superiority complex in men, and consequent inferiority complex in women. Both the sexes were happy till the Independence as each group lived in its illusion, accepting man as the Guard and women as the Guarded. But this unnatural setting received a jolt with the change that was wrought in the postcolonial Indian scene. Any changes in the society would reflect themselves in fiction. The scenario in Indian English fiction changed after Independence. Before Independence, the Indian writers in English belonged to either of the two groups: one, using English to intensify patriotic feelings in Indians to achieve freedom for the country, two, representing the existing social settings without any reference to the independence struggle. Now, the Indian English novelist began to write about wider issues that came up in free India.

The postcolonial writers of India freed themselves from political and economic issues which they left to the leaders of the county to deal with. The social, and more so the psychological, issues became their chief concerns. While most of the men writers were concerned about the inevitable changes in the Indian society in free India, some of them also dealt with the desirable changes in the Indian society to compete with the West. This competition with the west was not a compulsion but a natural process of being carried away by the contemporary Western literary trends. As has been stated earlier, several Indian writers settled down in countries like England, Australia, America, Canada etc. and were influenced by their surroundings. Inevitably, they wrote novels that depicted the contemporary trends. Postcolonialism, multiculturalism, diasporic writings, and issues related to race and ethnicity, feminism etc. form the literary world today. Indian English novelists show remarkable awareness of these issues and deal with them effectively.

Postcolonialism is a term which has replaced 'Commonwealth Literature' denoting the literature in English from those countries which once were colonies of the British Empire. The political connotations associated with 'Commonwealth literature' made the term unpopular as the writers and thinkers from the ex-colonies thought of themselves as free. A number of books published with financial assistance from the British council, symposia, conferences, seminars etc. created a movement like scenario of Postcolonialism during the last two decades of the 20th century.

The term postcolonialism was dropped recently and was replaced by 'New Literatures in English' African writers like Chinua Achebe, Ngugi wa Thiong'o, Buchi Emecheta, Caribbeans like Derek Walcott, Shani Mutoo, writers from the Western world like Sally Morgan, Robertson Davies and Indian English writers like Salman Rushdie, Shashi Tharoor, Amitav Ghosh, Bharati Mukherjee, Arundhati Roy and Allan Sealy, and others produced books which now are termed together as New Literatures in English. Bruce King, the noted critic of Indian English literature, has elaborated certain features of New Literatures in English in his book *The New English Literatures: Cultural Nationalism in a Changing World.* King's book offers useful explanation of terms like 'colonial experience', 'received literary tradition', 'cultural identity' etc.

The writers associated with 'New Literatures in English' adapt new strategies of narrative technique borrowing material mostly from the native tradition. This is an attempt to defy Euro-centric norms of criticism. They also use language different from the language of the Empire—combining native vocabulary, syntax, phrases etc. This has inevitably brought in the question of Nativism against Cosmopolitanism, more so with the Indian writers writing in English. But the narrative strategies adopted by Indian English novelists like Salman Rushdie, Githa Hariharan, Shashi Tharoor etc. should be convincing enough to show that they have their roots in the Indian soil. Their efforts to narrate the notion to 'others' should be appreciated. The debate regarding Nativism and Cosmopolitanism should conclude with the assumption that the two are complementary to each other. While retaining the native values, cosmopolitan outlook should be adopted in view of the fact that the national boundaries are getting dissolved into the global village.

Diaspora is an important event today when people are migrating across the continents for various reasons. The term has its origin in the dispersion of the Jews after the Babylonian captivity and in the Jewish communities that arouse after this dispersion. Today, Diaspora means dispersion or spreading of people originally belonging to one nation or having a common culture. It is a major social trend that affected literary creativity. Parsi writers like Rohinton Mistry, Farooq Dhondy and Firdaus Kanga, others like M.G. Vassanji, Bharati Mukherjee and Anita Desai, to some extent, contribute to the Indian diasporic writings. Multiculturalism, alienation and longing for the native past are the major trends of diasporic writings.

Contemporary Indian English fiction represents almost all the major trends in world literature today. Writers like Salman Rushdie, in fact have been acclaimed universally for their general artistic awareness and retaining the native values. Rushdie's *Midnight's Children* is unanimously considered postmodern classic which includes within its epic range all the major tendencies of contemporary writing.

Women's contribution to contemporary Indian English novel deserves to be mentioned separately. Kamala Markandaya, Nayantara Sahgal and Anita Desai belong to the first phase who initiated the process, each one of them opening different avenues. Markandaya depicted the East-West confrontation, Sahgal wrote political novels, while Desai explores the inner working of the female psyche through devices that are both modern and postmodern. The next generation of women writers includes Shashi Deshpande, Rama Mehta, Githa Hariharan, Arundhati Roy, Kiran Desai and others. Besides being concerned with the feminist issues, these women writers also show immense awareness of the general issues such as War, Violence, Communal Tension, Caste, Race etc.

The status of the Indian English novel is globally acknowledged as remarkable as compared to Indian English poetry—the genre which has given such stalwarts like Nissim Ezekiel, A.K. Ramanujan, Arun Kolatkar etc. Indian English novel has touched the pinnacle of international reputation. Indian English poetry, unfortunately has failed to perform similarly, maybe because this is not the age of poetry—but of prose and fiction which are capable of covering the larger issues of contemporary life and can face the challenges of science and technology. Indian English novel shows larger awareness of contemporary global issues. Salman Rushdie declares in *Introduction of the Anthology of Indian English literature* he edited with Elizabeth West that Indian English novel is India's only national literature represented at the global level, others being confined to local boundaries.

Anita Desai's contribution to contemporary Indian English novel is certainly impeccable. Born in 1937 during the British rule, Anita Desai produced novels related to the social realities of postcolonial India. She found that though the moral and intellectual spirit was based on rhetoric of equality, the socio-cultural issues did not conform to the construction of Indian nation. Yet another social reality was the problem of partition. Hundreds and thousands of lives were crushed and corroded; they had been the victims of cross-border conflicts; they found a place in the refracted pages of some writers. Jhabvala's *To Whom She Will*, Desai's *Clear Light of Day* and Hussain's *Sunlight on a Broken Column* bring dreadful memories of partition. Indeed Anita Desai creates a reluctantly compelling character, Ila Das in *Fire on the Mountain*, against the backdrop of this divided society.

Owing to the various governmental policies, the postcolonial situation in India produced a lively and eclectic, leisurely and affluent class of people. In fact, Anita Desai's *Cry, the Peacock* is a byproduct of the whims and fancies of the affluent society. She is the first woman writer who unfolds the dreadful experiences of strangulated lives. The emotion and sentiments, though baffling to the Indian reading audience, became an important part of the contemporary literary phenomena. Assimilating the postmodern conditions, Anita Desai's novels are a continuous search for human self. The characters suffer a kind of 'existential angst' to wrest some meaning out of it. They are like Camus's strangers. Adit in *Bye, Bye Blackbird* whose anglicized hatred for oriental race or longing for motherland defines an anti-representational character. The problem is the repudiation of culture; it is the problem of an unhealthy influence of an alien culture which deprives emotions and sentiments for their motherland. Desai's characters are caught in an existential predicament rooted in the awareness that death is the ultimate fact of life.[1] With loss of values and beliefs, the characters look out for death. Anita Desai perceives the conflict of the death by the domination of Time.

Desai's depiction of Time is—what she quotes on the last page of the novel, *Clear Light of Day*—a very significant line from Eliot's *Four Quartets*, Time is both a 'destroyer' and 'preserver.' Desai being deeply influenced by Camus, Kafka, Baudelaire.

Anita Desai's literary themes of identity, conflicting relationships, alienation, obsession with death and search for identity add meaning in life into her plots and characters. Her works usher in the necessity of encountering the effects of colonized cultures long after the imperial phase had ceased. Anita Desai made a place for herself in writing about the long-term effects on the psyche of women in the family and the society and their attitude, compromising or otherwise.

Desai's discourse is essentially on women. Like Melville, Anita Desai finds human dignity in little dark corners of life; not among the powerful and successful, but among the oppressed and the defeated; among the victims of God or of nature or of man or, simply of 'things.'[2]

Anita Desai interprets the reality of women in a postcolonial/postmodern situation as defeated and betrayed; exploited by fortune hunters; and those with the courage when they must say the great 'Yes' or 'No' to confront life creatively and unconventionally. Anita Desai unmistakably imprints a 'female sentence,' the 'female time' and quintessentially seeks self-realization and self-fulfillment as a female writer. Whatever be the subject, two types of women are portrayed by Anita Desai—the conformists and the non-conformists. These are very realistic human beings and not mere theoretical constructs.

Anita Desai is a genuine artist to the core who holds a mirror to nature. She does not recognize any theories of fiction but relies solely on her observation and experience. She thinks that the business of the artist is a realistic portrayal of what she sees and it is for the academics and the critics to analyze the creative art.

It is the "flashes" of vision, and a kind of "instinct" that lead the writer and not any theories. Anita Desai masters the art of the novel without making her works into social campaigns. She reflects on the condition of women and children in modern India and portrays them honestly in her novels.

Finally, the Indian English novel until the 1970s had a socio politico import with writers like Mulk Raj Anand, Raja Rao, Khushwant Singh and Kamala Markandaya. The exploration of the Indian psyche through fictionalized representations of poetry, music, art, life and at the same time the extremely deep, dark, destructive forces of life, conflict, sadness, alienation, ugliness that prevail through the individual experiences were taken up by the writers of following generation. This is what is exactly dealt with by Anita Desai. She captures the attention of the reader through the novels' intricate narration to follow a "particular consciousness," and brings the Indian English novel—into the mainstream of European and American fiction.[3]

So much is her commitment to English language that she creates typical characters with typical dialogue to catalogue a psychological drama of the mind. The study of the individual psyche and its interaction with social values create a psychic tension which forms the basis of postmodernist discourse. The postmodern discourse constructs its own language and adopts its own style against the established tradition. Here the novel's dense description of the characters' hypersensitivity, alienation, eccentricity enriches the artistic fabric. Also an associative use of landscape, myth, symbols, images of birds and animals reflect the mindscape. It is this meticulous practice, untried before, that places Anita Desai in Indian Writing in English in the dimension of postmodern art.

Anita Desai is not worried about the systems of social life; she is more concerned with the basic meaning of life and desires to arrange it into a credible shape. She comments on her own novels:

> My novels are no reflection of Indian society, politics or character. They are a part of my private effort to seize upon the raw material of life—its shapelessness, its meaninglessness.[4]

Born of the social and emotional milieu, Desai's novels are a representation of feminine sensibility that is caught in the crisis of a postmodern society—which is represented by the upper middle class of people,

> Who are not average but have retreated or been driven into some extremity of despair and so turned against . . . the general current.[5]

Whether Anita Desai came under the influence of the theories of existential concerns by Kierkegaard, Bergson, Augustine, Pascal, Heidegger and Proust or even Camus in the treatment of Time and Space is not certain. But the identity of women (and quintessentially of woman) that has moved away from family to society to social criticism in Literary Studies is given a new identity, a new liberty, and a new individuality. Her preoccupation with Indian women who are denied of their value and freedom, demands that her protagonists are new and different. Her women characters from Maya to Bim and immigrant women characters, Helen and Lotto grow in stature in terms of value and freedom. Triumphant and independent like her female protagonists, Anita Desai emerges to achieve what she wanted. Her universe needs no "masculine mediator," to explore her true potential.

A reading of Anita Desai's fiction gives a fair idea of the life in general and women in particular that we find in contemporary India. The discriminatory practices of people towards women, the consequent complexes of Indian men and women, their confused philosophy of life, the struggle of women to find their own identities—all find a graphic presentation in Anita Desai's fiction. A thematic analysis of selected novels of Anita Desai will further support the viewpoint that she is a powerful postmodern Indian writer.

NOTES

1. Rameṣh K. Srivastava, *Perspectives on Anita Desai* (Ghaziabad: Vimal), p. 18.
2. R.W.B. Lewis, ed., *Herman Melville* (Dell, New York, 1962), p. 12.
3. Lawrence, "Morality and Novel," Lodge, ed., *20th Century Literary Criticism,* p. 130.
4. Anita Desai's comments in *Contemporary Novelists,* ed. James Vinson (New Delhi: St. Martin's Press, 1972), p. 348.

5. Dalmia Yashodhara, An Interview with Anita Desai, *The Times of India*, April, 29, 1999, 13. Qtd. 'Introduction.' *Perspectives on Anita Desai,* ed. Ramesh K. Srivastava, p. xxiii.

Chapter III

Anita Desai: A Thematic Analysis of Her Novels

A thematic analysis of the novels of Anita Desai with particular emphasis on socio-cultural and economic background relates her content to the postmodernist issues. *Voices in the City*, *Cry, the Peacock*, *Fire on the Mountain*, *In Custody* and other novels exemplify this point of view. This statement from *Fire on the Mountain*, for example:

> One more sigh exploded from Ila Das. Isn't the world full of troubles wherever you look? In my village—it's the same everywhere.[1]

This is the essential state of life in the contemporary world. No one wants to see suffering; even if it is there, one wants to be insular. Everyone wants the world to become a better place to live. The above quoted lines present Anita Desai's vision of the world in which values, culture and civilization are in a state of total collapse in the post-Independence India. A novel is an initiation to talk. Possibly a dialogue could bring about an exchange and discussion on different points of view. At present, when the visual media like the cinema and the television turn the audience into passive viewers, it is the novel that can protect their imagination and increase intellectual productivity. Novelists present different points of view to enhance the discriminating power of the reader.

Just as a novelist can fire imagination of his readers, he can also defend the cultural destiny of a nation through his writing. Novelists give people a chance to reflect and talk about the reality of the subject. The future of the novel lies in its relevance to the nation. Novelists influence and shape attitudes of their readers, and create atmosphere for a specific purpose.

The writers offered some new and compelling insights into the expansive theme of colonial subjugation. The British attitude towards Indians brought a change in the socio-cultural economic outlook. The attitudes of the Indian men in Anita Desai's *In Custody* showed they were "intolerable," they wanted that "a woman should have a right to brain, talent, reputation and achievement." (196) In the same novel, one can see the intensity in the passionate voice of Nur's second wife whom Nur marries for intellectual companionship.

The message that Desai's novels convey to mankind is, that friendship, sincerity and integrity are illusions as they have lost their value. Society is multidimensional. There is immense diversity in it and we have to protect it possibly through the novel to bring about socio-cultural-economic change. A straight cut examination into the reality like the sigh exploded by Ila Das, "Isn't the world full of troubles" would give a chance to voice reality through fiction. The solution lies in raising the voice and doing "what we can."

No one can really get away from the voice of reality. The different perspectives of people struggling against the changing socio-cultural economic fabric of the nation are the expression through a voice. In such a fabric, it is the voice of the writer which becomes the voice of the nation. It is unique that Anita Desai's art comprises mainly powerful voices which become the leitmotif as the narrative unfolds. She, as a writer of contemporary reality, depicts the experiences of failure and defeat, the exotic and the irreconcilable, the fantasies and the pulls, the choices and the conflicts, the dreams and the desires resulting in the stifling loss of identity and meaning and leading ultimately to loneliness, desolation, suffering and annihilation. The living and the dead are voices that resonate all through Desai's novels. From personal level they rise to the local and then become a national narrative.

Art thrives on new talent and fresh voices. The theme of voices as a narrative device articulates the reality of the rising modern India connecting pre-Independence and post-Independence periods. Desai's impetus and ambition seem to create a medium through the voices which constitute a national discourse of socio-cultural economic class of the nation.

In Desai's novels, the subtle and significant turn of events by the characters expresses a sensitive search for a scheme. Her characters represent the symbolic themes of search for identity, death and annihilation as in *Voices in the City*, evasion and destruction in *Fire on the Mountain*, obsession, loneliness and awareness of death in *Cry, the Peacock*, failure to defend the dying Urdu language through Nur's poetry in *In Custody*, yearning for motherland in *Bye-Bye Blackbird*, escape and release from inauthentic domestic life *Where Shall We Go This Summer*. With redundant motifs of longings of men and women, fires on the mountain, cries of peacocks, caged artists, native blackbirds, false joys of routine life, estrangement of human relationships—all pulsate a crisis that deepens and darkens and offers a thick texture to the novels.

Voices in the City is Anita Desai's first novel. The story centers round Nirode and his sisters Monisha and Amla, who live in Calcutta entangled in a complicated web of defeat and disaster. Monisha's marriage to Jiban is a disaster leading to her suicide. Condemned to failure, Nirode tries to explore the depth of failure. He wants to cut the meaningless ascent of life to make descent straightaway. If Nirode is damned to failure, Jit is plagued with humiliation in life. Nirode is jealous of his mother's relation with Major Chadha. Monisha's death precipitates a death-wish in him. Her mother's arrival makes him feel the approach of Kali. He sees an amalgamation of death and life in the woman. Anita Desai's narration flows through several sensibilities into a meaningless riot of life and death.

Voices in the City is the voice of Calcutta and its principal characters. Desai depicts it as a unique society of self-obsessed people. The perpetual cry of all people is to end in annihilation; it is every Bengali's wish to be fulfilled. They are very protective about the socio-cultural norms and identify themselves with the urban class families of Mrs. Chadha, Jit, Mr. Ghosh, Prof. Bose and Dharma, and more emphatically, with the changing image of women like Mrs. Chadha, Sarla, Gita Devi, Monisha, Amla and the larger section of Bengali women who were active during the freedom struggle but relegated to ignorance after independence. The place of writers, painters and poets like Nirode, Dharma and David in such a society underpins the theme of struggle and failure in creating a meaningful life. The principal characters like to see themselves through the eyes of other people. Does Calcutta benefit them? To many it is a No, to some it is a Yes. Calcutta is the clay of design in the novel in which are pitted the lives of the principal characters.

Nevertheless this proto-colonial Calcutta is India's equivalent of modernism. The characters are progressive and have forgotten the history that happened in the early and mid-twentieth century. The city has elegant poetry, music, dance, manners, and graciousness of courtly civilization of the dying colonial power, which provide a stimulus to the Indian intelligentsia. Old Calcutta is steeped in crime, gutters, beggars, filthy roads, dirty buildings, disease, decay and darkness. Calcutta plays an important role from the dirty streets to the angry goddess Kali and the pure Ganges.

On analyzing the themes of Anita Desai's novels, one finds that the characters are caught in a complex socio-cultural economic crisis, where familiar routes of escape are shut off. The themes are interconnected and grow into a complex strand of experiences. The theme of loneliness is a pervasive theme in Desai's novels. Its complex experience like aloneness, forsakenness, friendlessness, lovelessness, rejection, reclusiveness, withdrawal, solitude, unsociableness, desolation, dissolution, dreadfulness, darkness, decay and death seem to haunt the individual, the family, the society and the city. This is a recurring theme in almost all novels of Anita Desai.

Voices in the City has a number of varying kinds of pairs but the relationship of all of them is characterized by alienation. Nirode's mother, a sophisticated accomplished and beautiful lady, has a useless drunkard husband who marries her for financial considerations. Consequently the husband turns malicious towards his wife and the wife seeks an escape and contentment in flowers and gardens. The relationship between another pair, Dharma and Geeta Devi, is a kind of passive suffering as she gives in to the wishes of her husband. Monisha, the sister of Nirode is confined behind bars and is surrounded by her husband's fat, secure, and placid uncles and aunts, and feels like a prisoner. A heightened awareness of boredom, monotony and lack of privacy always torments her. The love that is free of rules and obligations, complicity and stirrings of "mind and conscience," is beyond her reach. Even ordinary communication and understanding which is generally available to most human beings is missing in her relationship with Jiban. When, in her own house she is accused by her in-laws, of stealing her husband's money; her rightful expectation of support and moral help from Jiban is shattered by his heartbreaking sentence "that she should have told before she took it." She makes consistent attempts to withdraw from all material concerns of life and at a later stage discovers her life to be intractable, meaningless and uninvolved" which naturally amounts to nonexistence. Jiban learns to play only one role in his life and that is of the formal aesthetic, rigid bureaucrat. He fails miserably as husband, and is responsible for his wife's suicide. While Maya's husband Gautama at least occasionally tries to communicate with and understand Maya, and ultimately fails, Jiban has neither the will nor the capability to appreciate the sensitive world of Monisha.

Monisha's younger sister Amla is fascinated by Dharma, thinking him to be an ideal artist, and a man capable of understanding not only the conscious physical and spiritual needs of a woman, but also of reading the subconscious layers of the mind. In the beginning Amla thinks this relationship to be beautiful and satisfying; but her dream is mercilessly shattered when she comes to know that Dharma is actually a self-righteous, unfeeling zealot capable of turning his only daughter out of the house for having done something which he thinks to be unnatural and shameful. While turning his daughter out, he does not give even a thought to his wife and the suffering it would cause her.

The theme of alienation in *Voices in the City* is all-pervasive. Nirode, the protagonist of the novel fails to establish himself as a journalist. Instinctually he is a loner, for whom aloneness alone is the sole natural condition, aloneness alone the treasure worth treasuring. (24).He throws off every garment, fortune and family, and chooses rather to die of starvation than to go to his treacherous mother who has given in to the advances of Major Chadha. His mother's relation with Major Chadha leaves him embittered and he in turn embitters Amla's feelings for her mother.

David, Nirode's friend, derives great satisfaction in listening to Nirode theorize on anything. In Nirode's theory, Calcutta acquires a thematic character setting, the tone and tenor. Nirode can endlessly and compulsively talk of decadent Calcutta in

> malicious Bengali jibe . . . of lies . . . dark and demonic dreams that grovelled mostly with grossness of the city . . . various wild experiences, declaring them unique in one of his social class, little realizing it was the city that had thrust them upon him inexorably. (27)

To Nirode, Calcutta is an adopted city; indeed to his sister, Amla as well. She arrives in Calcutta to work as a commercial artist in an advertising firm. According to Amla, Calcutta is dead and does not notice her creep into life there.

Calcutta is deluged every monsoon, making survival impossible. The "uncooperative artists" and "cynical writers" make Nirode's journal *Voice* artificial and wasteful. His belief in *Voice* leaves him pessimistic. On the contrary, Prof. Bose who was born in Calcutta "needs the Calcutta earth, the Calcutta air" (58), though this air poisoned and killed his daughter.

To David's brother Sunny, Calcutta-wallahs were "spoilt urbanites" and different from the people of Babulpore. But David uses Calcutta to promote his business interests of exporting the Indian handicrafts and unfailingly celebrates its success in a great style with rum. Dharma is the voice of wisdom against the formidable terrain of Calcutta. Dharma and David are loners but never spell out their loneliness. To Nirode "their voices were broken and plaintive, their movements harried" (72) in the great current of life.

If Calcutta denied success, it appears to Nirode that David, Jit, Dharma, Sunny, Prof. Bose were all a pack of enemies, not friends; Mr. Ghosh sees in Calcutta the voice of dying colonial power that has lost all its courtly graces with the great beauties, Mumtaz Begum and Jahanara Begum. They were "no match to the South Indian silks in which women swathed themselves to-day." (80)

Sonny hated the "physicalness" of his father's (Mr. Ghosh's) generation who patronized "painted women." Verily, Mr. Ghosh cannot approve of the lethargy of the younger generation of Sonny that India might have to wait for another "conquering race to put things right for us." (81)

If Calcutta does not interest Nirode neither does Babulpore with "busy clerks" and its "Spartan functionaries." He feels himself like a clog in a machine to the uncontrollable happenings of the world around. We listen to an opposing voice in Jit to every new publication of Nirode's journal, *Voice*. Jit feels humiliated that Nirode had done it again. Rich and spoilt, Jit is a loner who suffers an existential trauma. Having married Sarla, a perfect upper middle class woman, in taste and style, he is humiliated by his wife who refuses to live with his parents whom he regards with great honour and respect.

Jit is an alter ego to Nirode. He is sick with his job and the intriguing activities that surround it. Nirode too feels humiliated and dramatically farcical to request his mother for financial help. The suspended issue of *Voice* and the vexing subscribers reduce his life to a mean wasteland. If Jit wishes to exchange his "humiliation" to seek Nirode's liberty, Nirode yearns for fame and good fortune.

REPENT AND BE SAVED—JESUS CALLS—is a blazing neon sign that Nirode sees emerging out of the pub with Jit, and it has a cathartic effect. It grows clearer into a voice that he should master the situation. Following the voice, Nirode offers to give up *Voice* to Jit so that Jit could lead a noble, academic and creative life. Ironically Jit is not prepared to risk his position, status or his wife, Sarla. Nirode flees from Calcutta to Monisha as it is not his land of adventure.

Jit's wife, Sarla has carnal appeal. Nirode dreads her presence and her sweet perfume evokes in him the fear of the death of Calcutta. Nevertheless, Calcutta's night bars were infested with "dancers and drunkards" with "sailors and prostitutes," "raucous and disreputable" people who would scream in "wild celebration" until the club goers fled.

According to Mr. Ghosh, Calcutta had a few emancipated young women like Mrs. Gupta "from Oxford" who used to play the game of tennis in "her white saree." Some Bengali women yearned to be modern like Mrs. Ghosh. They were a class of women who "did wake up a bit during the independence movement . . . but fell back to their old beauty sleep of neglect and delay and corruption . . . suppose it's a result of so many centuries of slavery to foreign rule." (81)

Gita Devi, the wife of Dharma, has the least obtrusive voice of women. It is full of piety, decorum and bears no conjunction to the likes of Sarla. Gita Devi will appear with "sweet dishes" and "thick syrup" or is heard saying her prayers in her kitchen temple of polished brass. (230-31) She is the basic voice of Dharma's actions.

Monisha marries Jiban, a jobless young man who is almost obsessed with family matters. Monisha is too transparent and vulnerable to such a stolid family of respectability and governmental security. Her tragic flaw is that her fallopian tubes are blocked and her problem is scrutinized by the household. Monisha cannot bear a child but she finds it more painful to bear the comments of others, like Gul the heroine of a short story by Amrita Pritam, who douses herself with kerosene, and dies. Monisha seeks to be alone "in privacy," "away" from the inspecting aunts, uncles, cousins, nieces and nephews. She is more comfortable alone and can work better. It is beyond her to listen to her in-laws discussing in loud voices about her "ovaries" and her "wardrobe."

When Kalyani De, her sister-in-law, throws open her wardrobe to find it full of books, Monisha is perplexed if there is anything to laugh at the books by Kafka or Hopkins or Dostoevsky or her Russian or French or Sanskrit dictionaries. Only Nirode can save her from this humiliation by taking her away into the jungles of Calcutta. Monisha is a misfit in Jiban's family who lives entirely on rice and rich sweetmeats and the security of government post and pensions. (110)

All day Monisha finds her voice suppressed. She cannot bear the uneasy lassitude of the people of Calcutta. She cannot understand why the celestial pair, Ganesha and Laxmi, God of fortune and Goddess of wealth, redeem the people of their ruthlessness. She finds compassion totally dead in the people and, their faces, dreadful and ghostly.

Jiban begs Monisha to be friendly, but Monisha cannot be like the Bengali women whose lives are spent waiting on men who are self-centred, indifferent and hungry. Women are always misunderstood by these men. Monisha finds it intolerable that the women behind bars of the windows were like caged birds, wounded and bleeding.

She wonders at the futility of their "who lives, eats, works, sings, bleeding through life?" (121) "To sort the husk, to wash and iron and talk and sleep," are the mundane duties of these women. That life cannot be lived beyond the "husk," is a mean choice of existence; an unproductive routine to Monisha.

Nirode falls sick again and again. The only way he feels is to stoically accept defeat. It is the absence of love that makes Monisha and Nirode "abject rebels" and craven tragedians. They are filled with dark, dreadful fear. They shy away from love and fear its attachment and desperately seek a release from life. In a way Nirode and Monisha are outsiders, exiles in society.

In the great drama of life, Monisha is accused of theft by her mother-in-law. It seems to her an absurdist's piece of action. She is confused and mystified to the point of exasperation. Unlike Jiban's mother Aunt Lila—Mrs. Chadha's half-sister—she is a woman of great spirit and believes strongly that a girl must have spirit and a profession. As she puts it, "a girl should be happy to choose her career especially in a country like India which, belongs to men . . . but it won't always be so, not when there are girls like you [Amla] and my Rita." (143)

Nirode gets reduced to a phantom and lives in a precarious state. Barred to see his aunt, Nirode meets Monisha clandestinely. The city of Calcutta turns monstrous gorging in "subterranean and stealthy" mortals like Nirode and Monisha. Amla fails to understand the cause of Monisha's change. She is puzzled at Nirode's wasted and alienated appearance. Ever since Monisha waved out of the window, her silent and barred agony haunts Amla. Even Aunt Lila cannot console her. Aunt Lila sighs to find the generation of Monisha diseased the younger generation diseased: "the very freedom we fought and gave you perhaps?" (179) It is Dharma alone who can make Amla's destiny shine and let her live it without sorrow. Amla too feels certain that it was Dharma who had held her taut, frightened face, that merciful magic mask, telling her in his cool voice to breathe deeply, to be still, to forget the pain (187) and remember a few things that Dharma tells to Nirode, about the intrinsically negative Calcutta.

Against such a foreboding, Amla sees Dharma "chivalrous," "subtle," "tender" and "prophetic." If this is so, she sits for a portrait not knowing what Dharma means to do with her portraits. Against the prevailing circumstances Dharma's genius over her paintings and portraits brings great success and joy. Nirode's voice of wisdom, Monisha's hidden voice on her smile, her mother's enigmatic "polish" or "balance" is a mystery to Amla.

Amla always wondered how Monisha had been married to the boring, ethical, self-complacent Jiban. It was beyond her courage and intelligence to extract any opinion out of Aunt Lila, who wanted Monisha to settle into a stolid and sufficiently educated family. Aunt Lila's earthy wisdom is that every girl must learn to find herself out. The mysterious power of Calcutta begins to work close to Desai's characters like Hardy's Egdon-Heath on its denizens. A.V. Krishna Rao thinks that the city of Calcutta is the invisible protagonist of the novel:

> Thus although one may be tempted to consider Nirode as the hero of the novel, the city of Calcutta is indeed the invisible protagonist of the novel. Calcutta, conceived as a force of creation, preservation and destruction is ultimately identified as a symbol for the goddess Kali.[2]

Calcutta begins its dance of death on Monisha. Monisha listens to a harsh, generous and vibrant voice from under her balcony. She shrinks to see the bewitching wild eyed singer making brusque movements of hands as a professional 'hermaphrodite.' The singer entertains a mystical communication to the crowd around her. Monisha stands apart while the others sway. It simply devastated Monisha's ears, with a wisdom that filled her with terror. It dawns on her that she won a war of mind while they lost a "war to instincts." Still it seemed to her that her victory was of more value than their loss.

The appealing exhibition of passion and voice make Monisha feel, as if her life was "sealed in a steel container" or "a glass cubicle," and "to live in it all her life." (239) She has lived it all. Smothered and stifled, she leaps to annihilate herself. She douses herself with the tin of kerosene and is engulfed by the black smoke balls of fire. It is beyond comprehension for anybody to understand "how it happened" and what had to be done.

The one voice that links the dreadful silence is Jiban's terrible admission of his fault "forgive me" but is abruptly eclipsed by the sympathy of Monisha's in-laws. It is Nirode, who alone understands Monisha and her death. He begins to see Monisha's philosophy in her death.

Mrs. Chadha arrives to voice "a farcical scene" of reunion. Amla discovers her mother's withdrawal, by her reiterated rejection through her glances. She appears as amalgamation of life and death to Nirode and Amla who has watched the sacrifice and is satisfied. "Mother Kali is the mother of Bengal . . . she is the mother of all, has given birth to us, she must also deal . . . our deaths?" (256)

Nirode, Monisha and Amla have been fighting their battle for the consciousness of knowledge and it is manifest that "Mother is all." Mother-Kali is the voice of "knowledge," "ignorance," reality, Maya, and birth and death. With Monisha's death, Nirode feels that he too is sentenced to death by Kali. The voice of Calcutta closes with the moving procession chanting the name of goddess to the beating of drums. Life is not living but moving towards death—this is the theme of *Voices in the City*.

The characters in *Voices in the City* are victims of socio-cultural economic forces at play. Monisha is a victim of social abuse because of her blocked fallopian tubes and stealing of money of her husband. Nirode is a social failure who fails miserably to voice his struggles. He is the voice of young India who wants to be different from the older generation and to establish an individuality of its own. He cannot accept his socially-flawed mother who can save him from his economic despondency because he is too egoistic to give in to his wealthy mother. Being a failure in life, he wishes to die.

David and Sonny are yet other voices of young India who believe that the present is founded on the past and, simultaneously, they welcome the changing economic patterns of family, property etc. David, however, does not like the generation of his father, Mr. Ghosh, who takes a happy refuge in the musical soirees, the rich cultural past which is a relic of the dying colonial power.

Amla moves with the socio-economic-cultural patterns of the society and appears a little emancipated compared to her sister Monisha. Mrs. Chadha is clearly the voice of modern India. Unlike her daughter Monisha, she does not consider herself socially flawed. Mrs. Chadha is successful enough to take the world ahead with her. Anita Desai is not interested so much in registering surface realities as in the probing of inner truths lying under the surface level. It is not the marriages, gifts, husbands, and wives that interest her, but it is the psychological drama behind all this. Thus, Anita Desai could be added to the list of psychological realists of literatures in English. This she herself makes explicit in an interview with Yashodhara Dalmia.

> One's preoccupation can only be a perpetual search . . . for meanings for value, for—dare I say it—truth. I think of the world as an iceberg—the one-tenth visible above the surface of the water is what we call reality, but the nine-tenths that are submerged make up the truth, and that is what one is trying to explore. Writing is an effort to discover and then to underline and finally to convey the true significance of things.[3]

Yet it is *Voices in the City* that foregrounds the thematic patterns enlarging the gamut of experiences and cutting across time and nation in the novels that follow.

Cry, the Peacock is another important novel of Anita Desai. D.S. Maini has rightly said: "*Cry, the Peacock* is typically a feminine novel, a novel of sensibility rather than of action. It has the quality of an orchid and of a flute about it. Its concern is almost wholly with the terrors of existence, and it achieves its effects through a series of exploding and multiplying metaphors."[4]

Maya, the hypersensitive, high strong and pampered, young protagonist, loves life sensuously. Colours, smells, sounds, feelings and emotions give meaning to her life and the world. Pets mean the world to her, while they do not mean anything at all to her husband Gautama. Her face is "round and childish, pretty and plump, pampered and smooth, silken with a 'small velvet mole'; small, shell-like ears, soft, overfull lips arched with vulnerable sweetness; long curled lashes and heavy, dark black brows could be a lovable face to many, but yet it is not a face that a man like Gautama could love. What Gautama sees in Maya mainly is unduly prolonged childishness; ignorance and silliness which he does not at all wish to indulge in. Maya's emotional, aesthetic and romantic needs are met with Gautama's practical hardness and lead to alienation.

Maya's sensuous needs are left unanswered by her elderly husband whose "bent spine," "projecting ribs" and a "papier-mâché face" shows that he is sexually cold and unattractive. There are literal and symbolic references in the novel to indicate Maya's physical needs being left unfulfilled and consequently leading to frustration and alienation. It is as though Gautama's eyes remained blank of appraisal to any response. In short, he sees "nothing less" or "nothing more." Naturally, it is difficult for Gautama, the lawyer, a man of reason, logic and practical worldly knowledge to understand the intensity of Maya's needs and bend down to her requirements.

Anita Desai's vision of the world as she voices through Raisahab, father of Maya, is that the "source of disintegration" is man's vanity in his power to act. Not realizing the futility of rebellion, man steers himself further and further "out of the orbit" in which he was born, and destroys himself. That the world is full of destruction is the Western theory of life, not an Asian one. It has been taught for generations that the merit of accepting one's limitations and acting within them is greater than that destroying them and trying to act beyond them. "One must . . . accept."[5] Inability of an individual to accept his own shortcomings is the theme of *Cry, the Peacock*. Maya cannot accept her own limitations. She cannot understand Gautama or grow to his level of argument. Raisahab and Gautama are spiritually enlightened characters who do not want to be attached to love and its inevitable baggage of unhappiness, depression and delusion. Their spiritual aspirations are far removed from the socio-cultural economic cries of the characters from voices in the city. Maya lives at a biological level. Desai makes an attempt to explore the submerged truth through the exploration of the psyche of her characters against her own vision of life, which is basically dark. The theme of the novel *Cry, the Peacock* develops on various levels of thinking.

Maya cannot be assured by her father's philosophy that what happens cannot be undone, and that all will be well soon to bring about the desired result. Raisahab, and his protégé, Gautama, can fight the current of life, and remain steady. The truth and philosophy of their lives is to accept their own limitations and act within them. *Times Literary Supplement* has recognized *Cry, the Peacock* as a lyrical novel. The novel is not an ordinary one based on the critical evaluations of the readers. The readers, no doubt, would have found it difficult to digest as the time sequence and space sequence were not followed in it in the Aristotelian sense of a proper beginning, middle and end.[6]

Cry, the Peacock is Maya's cry for her lover, Gautama, who is a disembodied, disconnected voice from another world. Maya is in need of a sharing human friend and a companion. Gautama's meagre love and scant understanding cannot fulfill her emotional needs. She submits herself to loneliness and to its occasional fits of nostalgia and hallucinations. Her loneliness cannot be filled by the blissful couplets of Urdu poetry or rise to the strains of music. She is haunted by the albino astrologer's prophecy. She cannot explain the prophecy of death to Gautama. It is this mysterious power that haunts her as a living death. Gautama is a disinterested intellectual totally out of element to help Maya. He is like a bogey-man who refuses to play with her. He understands her occasional breakdowns as a human need for vacation. Gautama is like Prof. Higgins in Shaw's *Pygmalion* concerned with Maya's transformation into a detached being.

According to Gautama, the path of life is beset with attachment, wonder, excitement, unhappiness, depression and disillusionment. Therefore one has to discipline one's life to hold it safe and secure. Maya cannot control her insane passions. She cannot see the fine evenings melt without fulfillment. Aware of death, and craving for love in life, Maya cries like the wild peacock. Her heart palpitates for others and weeps, knowing that their words are hers. Caught in the inescapable net where her father, brother or husband cannot save her, she pines for death. It is a wish fulfillment like that of Nirode in the voices. Maya is dying for Gautama's love. And what remains is guilt, delusion and irritation all convoluted into forms of loneliness.

Gautama's logic and faith are beyond her. Maya finds it horrible to accept the theory of karma, that—we may pay for what we may have done in our past life—that we might have done. (124)

The problem with Maya is that she had forgotten the "magic" of her father's words which once had the power to soothe and console. In the end, Gautama makes Maya see that the world she loves is fatal and despairing.

It was the panic-stricken death of Maya's pet, Toto that is the starting point of Maya's horror. The event prods her into an unremembered sorrow, as yet not even experienced. With the death of Toto, a kind of loneliness begins to haunt her. Childless as she is, Maya develops a "fanatic" attachment to the pet like an inevitable order of attachment. All day the body lay rotting in the sun which reminded Maya of the albino astrologer who predicted an unnatural death either hers or her husband's within four years of marriage. Gradually, this reminder of the prediction of death develops into a morbid obsession from which Maya is incapable of detaching herself. The obsession results in Maya's rapidly increasing psychic disintegration. Running parallel with the disintegration, is the stature of the albino who introduced as something indefinable, unrecognizable, "a strange" uneasy persistent haunting presence, that there remains hardly anything but him in the world of Maya. Even harmless creatures like domestic lizards and rats get metamorphosed into albinos in her private world.

It is fear of death that is the dominant note in this novel, almost all the objects and events are related to it in one way or the other. The novel not only begins with death and develops with an increasing obsession with death but also ends with it. The only difference is that, in the beginning, Toto's body was so dreadful to Maya that she grows hysterical; at the end of the novel it is insane that Maya herself hurls Gautama down the terrace causing his death. The paranoiac condition of Indian women even though they are liberated make them postmodern. Paranoia—a form of schizophrenia characterized by slowly progressive deterioration of personality involving delusions and hallucinations is an important trait of postmodernity. Maya, in *Cry, the Peacock*, suffers from this state of mind as she shares the contemporary reality. Violence, aggressiveness and death often produce paranoiac psychic condition and, eventually, make the character suffer. Maya suffers precisely from this psychic condition, so do several other characters in Anita Desai's fictional world. Anita Desai's art as a fiction writer, thus, moves close to postmodernism as a concept denoting the prevalent trends and tendencies of our times.

In a world characterized by loneliness and emotional insecurity, Desai's characters tend to be over-sensitive to violence and death. Violence, death and obsession with death figure predominantly in the thematic mosaic of Desai's fiction.

After Toto's cremation, Maya begins to suffer from an unknown fear. Every action of Gautama reveals to her his rational nature. He appeals to the reader's sensibility. He does not attach great importance to the "empty rites" of cremation. All through the novel, Gautama's voice rises to blissful and poetic expressions on the theory of detachment. As a true practitioner of the *Bhagwad Gita*, Gautama has words which are solidly simple and soothing. He enunciates the view that *Gita* does not preach involvement in tradition. It "preaches—rather recommends—detachment on every count." (17) His voice is sublime without the vulgarity of the ill-educated men or over-bearing women. Maya's need is physical companionship; she wants love which Gautama describes as follows:

> Love—that great splendid ideal of the young—ultimately becomes you will find for, the man a matter or dealing with bills that come in and for the woman, of worrying about them. (21)

Gautama will not reduce ideals to mundane superfluities for the sake of love, like Maya. The man has no use for flowers or stars. The spaces of the myriad stars above lurk with darkness, distance, separation and loneliness. Maya hates to see loneliness spread everywhere on earth. Contrarily, Gautama seeks for a star that has a heart capable of sorrow. All that Maya begs of Gautama is a single moment, an absolute happiness with Gautama to annihilate the torture of loneliness. She hallucinates a demonic creature deafening her ears with the dance of death.

The dance of death is the characteristic leitmotif of Anita Desai's hypersensitive characters like Monisha, Maya and Raka in *Fire on the Mountain*, who delight to set the forest on fire, and Nur in *In Custody* who emotionally breaks down over the dying Urdu language.

Anita Desai's characters are restless and want to be freed from inner anxiety. Thematically, all characters wish to escape from reality. The question "where" is an unsettled issue in terms of place and mind to the characters. Every novel holds a key to the other with an underlying pattern of action.

That Maya should be married to Gautama has been the prettiest ever superstition. As his protégé, Raisahab had great friendship and mutual respect towards Gautama and believed him to be the best companion to Maya. Raisahab always rejoiced in his daughter as a treasure. Maya's life with her father had been a fairy tale of good breeding, culture, leisure and comfort. Raisahab had much room for pleasure and discipline. Having grown in a bower of bougainvilleas and jasmine buds, Maya feels a lack of love with Gautama that no one loves her as her father did.

In Gautama's family no one spoke of love but always discussed affairs of parliament. Gautama's mother, an emerging socialite, is happy that Gautama is married to Maya, though Maya never understands if something was told, out of affection or with some motive removed from any personal feeling. (47)

Gautama's father is a freedom fighter, who having walked out of the cell, hopes to write a book on the villages and cities he had visited. Raisahab is the voice of the novel, and like the captain of a great ship, steers clear in the journey of life. Maya has not developed her faith in her father's doctrine of acceptance. She is yet to grow to understand Gautama's discerning knowledge of detachment. Harbans Singh, a friend of Gautama, tries to get Maya interested in palmistry. Gautama, however, opposed such things as "movements of the astral bodies—solids—rocks—or lives formed in the palms—will have the remotest influence upon our deeds and actions in our everyday lives" (79) can affect our lives. Maya's feverish ache is to experience "the ecstasy of being alive," (103) her dreadful fear that, if tomorrow I were a mere stone, mute, immobile extinct? For now I know my destiny." (103)

But a sympathetic gentle voice drifts her into a passionate prayer to bear the suffering, "Lord, thou dealt me so many sorrows, to bear them, couldst thou not also have lent me another heart?" (103)

Maya is vulnerable to sorrow with an excitable temperament and views things in a highly subjective way. She even seems to doubt her senses. All these signs indicate that her psychic disintegration is already on the threshold. Maya evinces not only the symptoms of schizophrenia but also of obsessive compulsive neurosis which involves thoughts and actions the individual recognizes as irrational but which still persist. Being a prey to such a disorder, a person is forced to think about something that he does not want to think about. Maya's neurosis lies in her persistent obsession with the albino and his forecast, despite the knowledge that all this could only be a nightmare. She is obsessively frightened also of the Kathakali dancers though she knows well that they are ordinary human beings like her own self. The difference in their appearances has been brought about only by the masks they wear.

Toto's death serves as a prelude to Maya's schizophrenia. With increasing disintegration of her psyche, the values and contexts attached to ordinary objects get muddled in her highly personal world. She sees everything in a subjective light which distorts reality.

Feeling one's body or actions to be those of someone else—a symptom of depersonalization—is also associated with schizophrenia. Maya starts evincing these symptoms gradually with her increasing psychic disorder. In the beginning it is difficult for her to recognize her voice as her own, but later we find her to be totally unaware of the way she speaks. Gradually, we find her becoming unaware not only of her manner of speaking but also of her speech until Gautama tells her to stop screaming. It is only through Gautama that the reader comes to know that Maya has been screaming, what she actually said remains unknown to the reader as well as to Maya. With the worsening of the state of depersonalization, Maya starts feeling her bodily organs to be separate from herself, and once reaches the point of feeling her to be a bodiless soul.

Maya's utter loss of hold on her own senses and the reality makes her a prey to hallucinations and delusions. Delusion in Maya's case finds expression in her obsession with the albino and his prediction.

Though Maya is aware of the fact that the albino's prediction is "a nightmare, no more" yet she takes it to be true—and therein lays her delusion. When Maya, without any external stimuli, hears a sort of rhythm and the beats which become louder and louder with her increasing insanity, she evinces the symptoms of hallucinations. The disintegration of Maya's psyche does not follow a straight line. Though from the very beginning of the novel she has been depicted as being on the brink of insanity, yet at times she behaves like a fully normal person and is even seen evaluating and analyzing her past and present with striking objectivity and directing the reader's attitude towards the incidents occurring in the novel.

Gautama has no realization how important sex is to life. He is an intellectual, and bereft of "impulses" and "coarseness" of physical love. Maya wishes his death subconsciously. The prophecy relentlessly and fatally competes with her. It is proved again and again that Gautama had hardly any love. Gautama's crystalline knowledge never sticks on Maya's mind.

> His orientation on love makes him, look like a 'mediator'—too fastidious to admit such matters as with its accompanying horror of copulation, of physical demands and even, overbearingly, spiritual demands of possession. (113)

Maya thinks so. Gautama would never be by her side. The odd thing about Gautama is that he was always with a "paper," or a "book" or friends because he feels that Maya is capable of finding greater peace alone. But, for Maya, life is impossible without attachment. The conflict between attachment and detachment is the theme of the story of Maya and Gautama.

Gautama cannot accept life as a single episode of "success and virtue," for they are too short and fleeting. To Maya action is important; otherwise life is an "amorphous darkness." Maya realizes that she is being punished by her Karma. She cannot be like Nila, Gautama's sister who—though unhappily married—dabbles with paints or engages in shopping and stuff with her mother. She overcomes her loneliness by trying to develop interest and find the pleasure in ordinary things of life.

The dominant theme of *Cry, the Peacock* is death. Maya is ever anxious to listen to Gautama's discourse on death and life after. Gautama cannot understand Maya's morbid desire and suspects if Arjuna's letter about his horoscope is the reason for it. Maya learns that, like her name, everything on this earth is an illusion. The only thing was to sleep with Gautama and put an end to the pretended sleep called life. Her pretended sleep is disturbed by the peacock's scream. As if arranged only for her agony, their scream becomes the agony of death of love with all order gone out of Maya's life. Maya becomes conscious of her great failure.

Cry, the Peacock is an oppressively fatal story of a married woman whose painful remembrance of past things is an effort to discover the inner meaning of life. Ever since their marriage, Maya and Gautama have never made an effective conversation. Their private and public life can never match the backgrounds of their everyday life. Subverting the traditional image of a woman and presenting new dimensions of women in family and society gives Anita Desai a distinct place in the postmodern world of writing.

Obliterating all her experiences, Maya looks for a release from the bondage of unfulfilled dreams. If Gautama's is an intellectual and spiritual pursuit through an educational experiment on Maya, Maya is driven by an incorrigible vagueness of the current. Maya ceases to be troubled over Gautama's return, his preoccupation, his distance become a part of the pattern that she at last accepted. (194). Maya feels infinitely sorry for Gautama—the slow, harmless and guileless being who walked the fresh grass and did not know he touched it.

Detachment being his armour he transgresses all sorrows. Yet, it was Gautama who had taught her the painful things of life when she was tortured by humiliating sense of neglect, fear, loneliness and desperation and gave her reassurance.

In the final scene, Maya hears the melancholic voice of the owl from the lemon tree. Gautama does not hear it and he remains silent, startled by her touch but mistakenly moves in between Maya and the gentle moon. Maya thrusts her arm towards him, into him and sees him fall through the immensity of air down the terrace. (208)

Maya sees no norms or values in society. She is a nonconformist with no pattern in her life. In contrast, Arjuna her brother rebels against the expectations of his father, the claims of his family and the standards of upper middle-class life. He is the type who prefers a bicycle when his father wants him to buy a car, and spends time in slums with lower class people, and makes friends with his own dhobi's son, Hari. He does all this because he finds life meaningless especially as lived by his father who follows all the social norms without any questioning. He is a kind of Nirode in *Voices in the City* who violates the social norms of the well-to-do middle class society in appearance and dress.

The nonconformist attitude of Mrs. Desai's characters shows that reality is unbearable to them. Therefore they want to withdraw from it. But withdrawal which does not come naturally to them, leads them nowhere. Ultimately there is the realization, that the path they choose hardly matters, life by itself is meaningless. Withdrawal contrasted with involvement figures most prominently in Desai's fifth novel—*Fire on the Mountain*. Life as seen by Nanda is dull, monotonous, insignificant, absurd and incompatible with privacy and individuality. Therefore she wants to withdraw from it. But the withdrawal, to which she resorts, is hardly capable of giving any meaning to her life. It is not a state of spiritual peace or the 'Nirvana' propounded by Gautam Buddha and symbolized by his bronze statue in the novel; but it is a state of "barrenness" and deadly "starkness," which is completely devoid of life, not because one has transgressed ordinary life to achieve a higher state of spirit but rather because one is withered and dead inside.

Nanda Kaul, wife of the late Vice-Chancellor, has had a life cluttered up with children, servants and guests all of whom had incessant claims on her. Though unwillingly, somehow she managed to live up to those claims, and conform to the roles and patterns assigned to her by society. Always dressed in silk saris and pearls, she bowed down to the requirements and status of her husband, but always felt that the pressure of the claims was much more than she could bear.

There had been too many guests coming and going, tongas and rickshaws piled up under the eucalyptus trees and the bougainvilleas, their drivers asleep on the seats with their feet hanging over the bars. The many rooms of the house had always been full, extra beds would have had to be made up, so that there was a shortage of privacy that vexed her. Too many trays of tea would have to be made and carried to her husband's study, to her mother-in-law's bedroom, to the veranda that was the gathering place for all, at all times of the day, too many meals, too many dishes on the table, too much to wash up after.

It is because she had too busy and meaninglessly tiring life that after her husband's death Nanda comes to Carignano at Kasauli, a lovely barren place. This act is rooted in annoyance, irritation and revenge, and a feeling of failure in not having been able to have a life of privacy, individuality, freedom and meaning. She wants to have done with all. Her only wish is to be left alone to herself. But it cannot happen. The postman comes and brings a letter. How much she may dislike it, the telephone bell rings. Despite her wishes, Raka her great-grand-daughter comes, and she has to embrace her. Nanda has to put in a great deal of effort to maintain her state of withdrawal. She finds it very difficult to appear not to exist. Moreover, though she identifies herself with pines and cicadas and wants to imitate death by being perfectly still, a continual and compulsive need to belong is always there stabbing her assumed stillness. That is why she is sometimes seen pining for contact. What pains her most is seeing Raka run after Ram Lal and swing from his arm. Complete withdrawal is unattainable and even that which is attained is found to be sterile and barren.

Though Nanda and Raka are alike to a great extent, in their reactions to communication, company and involvement, there is a subtle difference between the two:

> If Nanda was a recluse out of vengeance for a long life of duty and obligation, her great-grand-daughter was recluse by nature, by instinct. She had not arrived at this condition by a long route of rejection and sacrifice—she was born to it simply.[7]

Raka—the born recluse is happy in her world though it consists only of broken, devastate and appalling objects. Withdrawal comes to her naturally. Whatsoever she does, she does out of her own will.

She is the perfect model of what Nanda falteringly tries to be. But like Nanda's withdrawal, Raka's also is not in a spiritually transcended state like Gautam Buddha's detachment or 'Nirvana.' It is a morbid state of rejection of the unbearable reality of her father's filthy abuse, as several unsavoury incidents always hover in Raka's mind.

It is but natural for the off-spring of such a reality to be a perfect recluse and a model of morbid withdrawal. She instinctively shrinks from company, society and its culture. Loneliness never bothers her. This type of withdrawal again can hardly be expected to give any meaning to life. The only thing she can ultimately do is to set fire to the world around.

Involvement gets embodiment in this novel in Ila Das—a social welfare officer—bold and energetic, fighting for the betterment of existence. Even though to provide herself with the bare minimum is difficult for her, she seems to be happy, loves life and people both, and tries to maintain the dignity of her father who was a rich well established man. But she is raped and mercilessly murdered, proving the meaninglessness of all she did. Ila's involvement provides a sharp contrast to Nanda's withdrawal. If a telephone ring is extraordinarily ominous to Nanda, for Ila it is a wonderful change to communicate with people. Raka's arrival is a great calamity to Nanda; but, Ila on the other hand can't bottle herself up any longer. These contrasting attitudes highlight Desai's vision that everything—withdrawal or involvement—is equally meaningless.

Cry, the Peacock presents a tension where Maya subverts the tradition. In the process she becomes an outsider not conforming to the role of woman. She is clad with something catastrophic. The novel portends the theme of death clouded with mystery. Though Anita Desai gives a satisfying end, it is intractable whether Gautama's death is an accident or effected consciously by Maya. After the death of Gautama, Maya moves like a haunted woman. Nila watches Maya playing with toys, like a child. Nila distrusts Maya's innocent game of the toy soldiers.

It is Anita Desai's belief that Indian women are traditional and find it difficult to break away. Gautama's mother's plea is that less the people see and hear Maya's story, the better. In Anita Desai novels, the problems of estranged self project reality through artistic parallels more powerful and eloquent than common collocation of novels.[8]

It is the story of a private tragedy of Gautama's mother and the cruellest reality of Maya is evacuation to an asylum. The cruel realities of feminist voices were beginning to appear as the critical and interpretative dimension of postmodern writing. While *Cry, the Peacock* introduces complex and emotional states of alienated self, it even offers a comprehensive critique to the various themes of the novels that follow.

The theme of loneliness continues in the novel *Fire on the Mountain*. Nanda Kaul can be said to be only crazy for trying to attain complete withdrawal which is not attainable, but she is certainly not needed. Anita Desai's characters are lonely and incapable of love. They withdraw from reality. The lone voices of Nanda Kaul, Ila Das and Raka do not like to establish any order of contact with the outer world because they have failed in their effort. The socio-cultural trends outside obstruct them from bringing any change in the existing order. Nanda Kaul cannot understand the inability of her upbringing to comfort her children—that children were all "alien" to her. She neither understood nor loved them. She lived at Carignano by choice because that was what she was reduced to doing. Nanda Kaul does her familial duty out of vengeful obligation. Victim of the changing cultural patterns of her family, Nanda Kaul wants to be done with all letters, messages, demands and requests, promises and queries.

Asha's meddlesome ways and her granddaughter's helplessness are all too much for Nanda Kaul. She has discharged duties and does not like to be dragged into them again. At Carignano she wanted no one and nothing else and whatever else came or happened would be an unwelcome intrusion and distraction to her. The barrenness of Carignano with its close apricot trees seemed completely satisfying. Her great granddaughter's arrival at Carignano seemed "hard and unfair."

Raka, the great granddaughter of Nanda Kaul, is like "an uninvited mouse or cricket" (80) at Carignano. Raka "hated nurseries," childhood illnesses, milk, medication and "certainly the parks of cities never gave her the necessary pass, the key to freedom and excitement. She seeks freedom at Carignano. She was hedged and stifled by the words and dreams of her great grandmother. Nanda Kaul deludes the girl only to win some love from the girl. Raka likes to go up the hills at Kasauli and set the forests on fire. She is a troubled child, is haunted in her sleep by her crying mother. She has a morbid desire for a destroyed house, especially a burnt house, and derives great pleasure in seeing "illegitimate," "uncompromising" and "lawless" things. Raka is a product of the failing cultural values of upper middleclass families in modern India. The images of sight and sound reinforce the theme of loneliness. Raka was an utter "misnomer" of the calm and shining moon; she is always jumping around and annoys Nanda Kaul. Nanda Kaul finds Raka despairing and indeed not a part of her. Raka wanted to pursue her own secret life among the rocks of Kasauli. Nanda Kaul always felt that Raka had a "genius of disappearing" and gift of avoiding what she regarded as dispensable. (63)

Both Nanda Kaul and Raka are restless and look for release. Nanda Kaul discovers that Raka is hurt by the sight of "caged animals." This gives her a cue to beguile the child. Nanda Kaul beguiles Raka with words and dreams, but never misuses Carignano. Carignano had to be kept clean, true and open for the wind to blow.

The house of the Vice-Chancellor was a hub of intense and busy with friends of all ages, sizes and families. After her husband's death, the sons and daughters packed their belongings and escorted their mother to Carignano. Raka was an "outsider" whose presence oppressed Nanda Kaul horribly. She did not want to be drawn again into the child's world. (45)

Raka was perceptive and loved the darkness. She hated to see people especially the cantonment revelry which reminded her of her father's home that made Raka wet her bed. The harsh abuse and her mother's crying threaten her like a fire in a dream. It arouses a desire to set the forest on fire. Her fire has been interpreted in many ways. As critics have pointed out—Varieties of loneliness in *Fire on the Mountain*, provide a whole set of hypothesis.[9]

Ramlal rouses greater friendship in Raka than her great grandmother especially with his stories of the devil and hubshee. Nanda Kaul's talkativeness becomes unbearable to Raka. Surprisingly Ila Das enkindles some love in Raka which Nanda Kaul has not done. Nanda Kaul feels she should invite poor and helpless Ila to stay at Carignano. Ila Das's belief "that the women were willing to try to change but the men were hard to be taught—leads her to resign to the situation that one must simply shoulder responsibilities and do what one can." (132)

Caught in the socio-economic tide with a desire to reform the society, Ila Das stumbles down. Her fate is doomed by Preet Singh. Her efforts to stop Preet Singh's child from getting married hits her in the worst form of cruelty. Preet Singh rapes her until she is finished and broken. Nanda Kaul, Ila Das and Raka are in need of love. The socio-cultural economic forces are far greater than their individual fights.

The theme of struggle and sacrifice to save the dying Urdu language is against the socio-cultural-economic forces which is the major preoccupation in the novel *In Custody*.

> Before Time crushes us into dust we must record our struggle against it is the voice of the greatest living poet, Nur. We must engrave our name in sand before it [wave] comes to sweep it away and make it part of the ocean.[10]

Again and again the socio-economic-cultural forces bind ordinary man or poet into an illusory trap from which there is no escape.

Abid Siddique, Head of the Department of Urdu of Lala Ram College, lives in a decayed historic house that is open to bazaar. Ironically, it is an open trap for one and all to join. In the movement of the action, Siddique's monetary offer to Deven to capture Nur's voice; makes him wonder, if the whole enterprise was a trap set by Murad, Siddique or by Nur and his wives. (143)

The mission to immortalize Art—Nur's poetry—in an age marked by science and technology appears observed. Deven realizes that the "evils of technology" were an interruption to art. According to him, technology has freed man from the law of gravity and sent him to space but made a 'steel trap'; and the soul of a poet will not rise and float to be caught in a box.

That man was also a victim of the technological failures in the new age of Electronics is an interesting sub-theme in the novel. Poetry cannot be "created at asking" as if a poet is "ground between stones" or would bleed in order "to produce poetry." (153) Art must have a purpose to resolve the socio-cultural economic problems of society. Hence the need for Art is to be in custody and the novel is a search for fulfillment of this need. If Nur's poetry gives "safe custody" then Deven was the custodian of Nur's poetry, "spirit and soul." Conversely Nur was the custodian of Deven. Art in custody would give Deven strength to face the calamities in life and Nur would overcome his social and economic problems. The sublime truth is that timeless and spaceless poetry of a dying language has to be preserved against the circumstances that are hostile to Arts in contemporary times. In fact, the time is marked with challenging concept of art which again is an important postmodernist feature.

If "language has to be served," it needs a "life time dedication" (16) according to Deven's friend, Murad. Everybody writes poems but it cannot be accomplished by many is the contention of Murad, the editor of *Awaaz* and the antagonist of the novel *In*

Custody. "No special issue on Urdu poetry would be complete without the verses of Nur," (16) declares Deven. Murad prevails on Deven to do a full-length feature on the dying poet, Nur before he is gone. Deven finds it possible considering his socio-economic status. To him the entire world was a cruel trap, and Deven lived in a strip of no man's land, which was in a state of desolation. He was always trying to find a way to reconcile the meanness of his physical life with the purity and immensity of his literary yearnings. Deven fears that the journey might be a disaster. He feels that he had neither the experience nor the confidence. Having arrived at the house of the greatest living poet Nur, Deven gives Murad's letter of introduction. Deven feels a tide of jubilation rise on being invited into the presence of his hero. It was as if God had leaned over a cloud and called for him to cone up, and angels might have been drawing him up these ancient splintered stairs to meet the deity. (39)

It was another realm that could grasp him from his "disordered, hopeless" life to "a domain of poetry, beauty and illumination." (40) A poet with "such God like magnitude" ought to have been presented with "a prayer" or "petition," thought Deven and anxiously conveys his purpose to Nur.

Another dominating theme of the novel is the colonization of Hindi Wallahs. This was a different type of colonization practised by the "congress-wallahs" to set Hindi on the top in order to rule India. It is a different type of colonization practised in modern India. While the old poet cannot understand the aspirations of a temporary lecturer from Lala Ram Lal College to preserve Urdu language, Deven recites a few lines to show his appreciation and the need for the preservation of Urdu language and its culture.

The artistic process is not a continuous process and artists are an unpredictable race of species whose whims and fancies cannot be understood by inadequate and inexperienced people like Deven. The fantasy of listening to the poet barely begins when Nur is surrounded by "clowns, jokers and jugglers" who fill him with drink and greasy biryani. And everyone speaks with artistic excesses as if from a pure "Indian camp" or "Pakistan camp" or "pure-Persian camp" and the demotic, Hindustan camp.

To the poet, the matter was not "Pakistan and Hindustan, Hindi or Urdu," it is the "concept of time" (54) and its perspectives. Nur conceptualizes that he loved poetry not because it made things immediate but because it removed things to a position where they became bearable; where Pakistan or Hindustan or Urdu or Hindi were all accepted. Poetry had the power to deal with frightening and inexplicable experiences like time and death to a point where it could be studied safely. When Deven's dream interview turns into a nightmare, he feels pained that the whole thing was simply not real, but a humbug. At least Deven had his poetry to redeem, but Sarla was "plain" and "pessimistic" and never tolerated social or economic failure. It had added accusation and bitterness to Deven's life. Compared to the horror of the dangers of Nur's poetry, Deven wishes to exchange it for the undemanding chatter of his child.

It is actually Murad who had dragged Deven out of his job to get work as secretary to Nur. And now it was for Deven to have Nur's memoirs on tape to transcribe them at leisure. (92)

With no worthwhile Urdu being published, Abid Siddiqui, Head, Department of Urdu, expresses a need for Urdu poems. According to him: "If Nur Shahjehanobadi's poetry was forthcoming after a passage of fifteen years of silence, it will be a great event in the small world of Urdu poetry." (111)

He welcomes the prospect to the Urdu departments that the libraries could boast of tapes of the poets who will become singing birds and usher colleges into the era of electronics. Nur was the "rage in Delhi," he was a magical name. The honour is owed to Deven. Deven is happy that it was not Nur's name that was bringing about this transformation; it was his genius, his art that he was going to give Nur's poetry to posterity. Now Deven had to capture and preserve that art for posterity. He has been allotted a significant role in life. But Nur protests to record his words like in cinema for songs. This is a cultural shock to Deven. He regrets his lack of ability to do it professionally and undertakes it as some dilettante's self-indulgence. He can't withdraw, for it is too late. Deven wants to write the memoirs of Nur for *Awaaz* if Nur could speak or recite to a few questions about his life, work and ideas. After listening intently to Deven, Nur shakes his head seriously, that Imtiaz Begum does not like him to recite any more.

> I am forbidden. You don't understand. She is right—absolutely right—I only make a fool of myself—an old man, my day is over laugh, feel bored; they want someone new and young, you see. (115-16)

Deven becomes furious that Nur has not understood how people loved his poetry. The whole exercise of holding the interview or getting the tape-recording seemed futile to Deven. He realizes that Nur is in the custody of his "wife, wives." Their motives of jealousy and vengeance inhibit Deven to complete his task. Besides, a pathetic resignation and helplessness capture the old man.

Nur falls to his wife's appeal throwing Deven berserk. The old wife accuses the new wife as a witch planted in the house of Nur. Nevertheless the older wife offers to help Deven to let Nur escape from the trap door for a payment. It is an economic obligation for Deven that he can't escape as put by Nur's older wife. "You think he has no family to feed? Are poet and poet's families to starve." (126) The crude speech is a blow enough to Deven. He sees that the poet is in the custody of an uneducated wife that he will have to perhaps abandon his project.

The "jealous tigress," Imtiaz Begum has already confused the old man. She accuses Deven of deceiving the "poor weak man." I have made my inquiries, she said:

> I know your kind—of jackals from the so-called universities that are really asylums for failures, trained to feed upon our carcasses. . . . Now you have come to tear at our living flesh. (118)

If Nur was in the custody of his wives, Deven was a trapped animal. In his youth, he had had the illusion of having free will, not knowing that life is a trap of marriage, family, job, etc., now there was no way out of it.

But Abid Siddique offers to procure more money from the authorities to help Deven. On an agreement from the Principal to release funds for payment, Deven seeks one week's leave. But after some arrangement over the payments is made, the enterprise fails. Chiku's poor assistance misses Nur's recitation. Deven tries a second time but discovers that

> Chiku was fast asleep with the tape recorders on doggedly recording all Nur's abuses and expletives. (115)

Chiku's ineptitude, the heedless idlers deflect Deven's task. Nur asking for interval of meals and drinks frustrates professional enterprise of Deven.

While it is an alarming loss of time and money with Chiku's rising charges, Nur declines Deven's idea of shifting and selecting from the "debris" of the poet's lives. He firmly refuses to proceed with Deven. Not being able to overcome the severest damage to Urdu poetry, Nur curls up in bed like a child. Deven finds all the exercise a fiasco. The tapes, recorded so far, do not produce a single sound. He realizes that the tapes that he had picked up were hopeless and, in addition, the equipment was bad. Murad wants the tapes. Deven is very annoyed not at completing the assignment entrusted to him. Deven makes great effort to describe Nur, as the greatest and the best poet.

Another colleague comforts Deven and offers to edit the tape and capture the single voice of Nur. The project is an obvious failure. Further the "patchwork" done by the boys to put it together becomes completely useless from a scholarly "point of view." All that Deven succeeds is to give a "monograph" for the funds actually meant for tapes. Siddique describes the tapes as a "total disaster" and of "no value." Deven feels he was fooled because Nur had not told him he wanted to be paid.

The truth that comforts Deven is that he was sincere and respected the poet purely for the love of his poetry. The voice of Nur assures that "when the last of my pigeons is gone, I will cease to write poetry for ever. I will go with them." (200)

Deven's alliance with Nur's poetry was an unending burden of muddles. Deven is not a custodian of Nur's poetry but a cultural ambassador whose struggle is to preserve Urdu language through Nur's poetry. This is worth a study of thematic significance. While everything sounds simultaneous, the reader has access to Deven's perception of mind. Anita Desai's opinion of art of writing employed in the novel is: A writer does not create a novel by observing a set of theories—he follows flashes of individual vision.[11]

Thus Desai shows, in *In Custody*, the dialectical tension between "reality" and "fantasy" that becomes her major preoccupation. The side of "reality" is heavier, and ultimately wins over "fantasy." It entangles the protagonist Deven in its powerful grasp so tightly that ultimately he has to bend to compromise with it. Besides the demands of his job, he has to look after his wife Sarla and son Manu. His world of reality is full of financial problems, tensions between him and his dissatisfied wife, and the obligation of his job which he finds difficult to face with his timid nature and lack of confidence. To escape from this real world, he searches for a world of fantasy which consists of hopes of confirmation and promotion in the college, fame through successful accomplishment of his literary projects, cultivation of his love of poetry, and procurement of money.

Whenever the world of fantasy allures Deven into its realm, the forceful grasp of reality brings him back. Each time he returns to reality, he is comparatively more disheartened, and gets entangled deeper into problems. Ultimately he has to compromise with dull, drab, monotonous, mundane reality, as his attempts to escape into a world of fantasy result in total disaster, leaving him broken to face the assaults of existence. It is the dismal reality that gives the dominating colour and tone to the novel. Fantasy may gleam now and then but ultimately it leaves the scene as dark as before. Postmodern fiction is not all about technicalities. It also depicts the socio-cultural conditions that control individual lives. Men and women live in an atmosphere where distorted facts send them into fantasy. What results ultimately is a bizarre, strange world inhabited by these men and women. This is not the Freudian world of 'unfulfilled desires' identified with 'modernist sensibility' but the 'postmodern condition' wherein personalized lives and social relations are affected by the threatening forces outside, often in the form of death and violence.

Sita's withdrawal in *Where Shall We Go this Summer*? lies in her leaving her conformist husband, home and society behind and leaving for the island, Manori. Sita rejects the existing normal patterns of life in order to withdraw to the island Manori where she thinks that the magic created by her father twenty years ago might help her to fulfill her will of keeping the fetus in her womb safe from all threats of destruction. But when she finds that there is no magic on the island to help her, she returns to the normal patterns of life. If Sita withdraws to the island Manori, Maya in *Cry, the Peacock*, withdraws to her subjective world to her gradually increasing fears of death. In time, Maya's withdrawal results in total psychic disintegration from which she is never able to recover.

Some impersonal forces like locale also make Desai's characters withdraw from life, or to react to it in a particular way. In *Voices in the City*, Calcutta is made to serve not only as a befitting background against which meaninglessness and absurdity can be explored, but an attempt has also been made to make it function as a force and an agent that renders life meaningless. Hence Calcutta transcending the role of a locale against which the theme is presented, becomes a force, a theme in itself.

The sordid, ghastly, monstrous force of Calcutta gets identified with the goddess Kali. It preys upon people, renders their lives worthless and finally swallows them up totally. At the end of the novel *Voices in the City*, we see that Monisha gets swallowed up by Calcutta while Nirode is under the torture of an agonizing feeling that next, it is his turn. In the beginning Amla, one of the most cheerful characters ever created by Desai, finds it highly exciting to reach Calcutta and to drive through the Dalhousie Square with all its red gingerbread houses, domes and cupolas and pigeons. She loves driving also into Ballygunge and sees the weather-beaten mansions and palm trees. But the dark, devilish force of Calcutta does not take long to make Amla realize that this city conspires against all who wish to enjoy it.

The maladjustment of the coloured immigrants in Britain and the vice versa difficulties of NRIs in India, exist as an uncompromising subject of debate and issue. Anita Desai highlights the conditions that create this situation in her novel *Bye, Bye Blackbird.* In *Bye-Bye Blackbird* also to some extent, Anita Desai seems to have intended to render locale as a force, exerting pressure on the characters and affecting their attitudes. In the beginning Dev, who reacts against everything that is English, is shown to have been so influenced by the spirit of the place that he gets infatuated by it, and becomes prone to ignore all the insults thrust upon him by the English. On the other hand Adit, who was well satisfied with his life in England, was proud of having adopted English taste and ways of thought, is disenchanted and leaves for his native land. The authorial voice somewhere, at some point finds England's green and gold fingers let go off Adit and clutched of Dev instead. England had let Adit drop and fall away as if she had done with him or realized that he had done with her, and caught and enmeshed his friend Dev. It was as though this were an arbitrary act of England's abstract law to which Adit and Dev had quite unwillingly succumbed.

The major thematic focuses of Desai's three novels *Clear Light of Day*, *The Village by the Sea* and *In Custody* are different from those favoured in her other novels—they, therefore, deserve separate treatment. In *Clear Light of Day*, it is mainly with the force of time that she deals, and in *In Custody* the main cancer is the grasp of mundane reality from which there is no escape. The *Village by the Sea* being a novel especially for children deals with the miseries caused by poverty, and seems to be giving an advice to adapt oneself according to the changing times.

Regarding the theme of *Clear Light of Day*, in an interview with Ramesh K. Srivastava, Desai observes:

> In my new novel, *Clear Light of Day*, I have tried to construct a four-dimensional world, the fourth dimension being Time. I wanted Time to have as palpable an existence as the spatial world perceived by the five senses. I wanted time to be an element like light or darkness, that is pervasive, and that is perceived by the characters as music is heard, scents smelled, food tasted, texture felt, sights seen—a part of their everyday consciousness. . . . What I have tried to prove is that although time appears to damage, destroy and extinguish, one finds instead that nothing is lost, nothing comes to an end, but the spiral of life leads as much upwards as downwards and is in a perpetual circular motion, both the past and the future existing always in time present.[12]

Entangled in the spiral motion of the passage of time, the characters of *Clear Light of Day* succeed in fulfilling some of their ambitions and fall in respect of a few others. But in every success there is some inherent failure and in every failure there is some hidden success. Bim succeeds in being highly educated and in being independent. She has succeeded in her determination to help Tara, Raja Baba and Mira-masi, and has also achieved her aim of living alone and not getting married. But in the process of gaining all this, she has lost a great deal in terms of love, marriage and children. She lives in the house in which she was born, and teaches in the college she herself was taught. Having been introduced to us dressed in a shabby, dull, home-made gown in contrast to Tara's elegant pale blue one, she seems to be living a dull stagnant life. Unlike Bim, Tara is married and well off, she is a mother of sophisticated children, and wife to a well groomed, well-informed officer in Foreign Service. She has travelled wide and has seen many countries while Bim does not go even to New Delhi often. Yet in terms of independence and individuality she is a loser. While eating an ice-cream cone offered to her by Bim, she is afraid of having been seen and scolded by her husband Bakul. At seeing a guava falling in the orchard, though her mouth tingles to bite rough hard flesh, she dares not eat it because of the fear of being criticized by her highly sophisticated children. Rich, widely travelled, and satisfactorily married (unlike most couples of Anita Desai), Tara is jealous of Bim who is handsome. All the men seemed to acknowledge this and respond.

Raja gains in having been able to marry Benazir—the daughter of his childhood hero Hyder Ali. He is successful not only in adopting Hyder Ali's life style, but also in acquiring his entire property. His heart is brimful with content when he sees his little son—Riyaz dressed like a Persian prince, riding on a milk white pony, just as Hyder Ali himself did. But the process of achieving all this makes him lose his heroism, his vocation, his own identity and individuality. He ends as a fat rich man, living a life of pomp, show and vanity. Instead of being himself a hero, he becomes a weak and banal imitator of a person whom he admired in his childhood. Thus the spiral motion of time leads these characters as much upwards as downwards.

The preserving aspect of time can be seen in the process of growing of the Das children from infancy to childhood and from childhood to adulthood. It is due to the passage of time that Bim is able to forget her grudges against Raja, to forgive him and to reestablish the severed relations. When Tara repeatedly refers to the incident of bees swarming round Bim in the Lodhi Gardens, and her own running away, leaving Bim to the mercy of the bees; she finds that time has made Bim forget almost everything about it. As Bim hardly has any comment to make, there is no question of giving or asking for forgiveness. Time not only makes them forget their grudges and help them maintain their sanity and psychic wholeness, it also helps them in a thousand other ways. Raja—a TB patient—regains his health with the passage of time. The communal riots of the partition get settled with time. Moreover, all the characters are able to fulfill their ambitions only through the passage of time.

It was the destructive aspect of time that changed Raja from a healthy, energetic, fiery and dashing young boy to a weak and pining tubercular patient. Aunt Mira grows shabbier and skinnier and seedier with the years. Having been affected by time, Bim's mother—an ageing, graying diabetic woman gives birth to congenitally handicapped and mentally retarded Baba who can lead a life only of perpetual childhood. Even inanimate things are not safe from the destructive aspect of time—and are affected and ruined in due course.

The passage of time in the novel has been shown as affecting every aspect of life—the physique of people, their awareness of things, attitudes to various objects and persons, and even the roles that people play in family and society. Raja changes from a loving brother to Bim into the exacting landlord talking of the issue of raising the rent of the house in which they had both spent their childhood. When Mira-masi comes to the Das family, Bim, Raja, Tara and Baba—all of them are children. They seek love and protection from her and get all that they need. But in due time, the children grow up into adults and Mira-masi gets reduced to the state of a "swaddled child." The only difference is that she now intensely longs and pathetically asks for a bottle of whisky instead of milk. The significant change that sets the attitude and liking of Bim with the change of time is noticed by Tara with reference to Raja's poetry. Tara knew, "that Raja was a poet and wrote great poetry," but now Bim, his favourite sister, finds his poetry banal, nauseating, terrible, imitative and repetitive.

It is not only time that affects and changes people. The characters too react actively against the flow of time. Congenitally handicapped Baba seems to be living in the same time. Tara is so preoccupied with her past and her childhood that she is not able to accept any change brought in by time. Until the end of the novel Bim cannot adapt herself to the demands of the changing times, and wants to check its powerful flow. It is only in the end that she changes. In this novel, it is only Raja who goes along with time.

The Village by the Sea deals with poverty and misery at the material level. Unlike other novels it has little to do with philosophical, psychological and existential concerns. Anita Desai might have deviated from the norm she set herself in her other novels because this one is speçially written for children, which accounts also for its remarkable lucidity, simplicity and concreteness. The chief protagonists are two rustic children—illiterate, naïve-thirteen year old Lila and twelve year old Hari—having a seriously anemic mother, a heavily drinking father and two small sisters—all needing to be looked after—all swamped in poverty and misery.

Needing a job desperately, yet having hardly anything to do, Hari can indulge himself only in things like whistling, sitting idle and filling his hands with fistfuls of sand or picking up pebbles to toss from one hand to the other. Having no particular training or qualification enabling him to earn money, he is in a desperate state of hopelessness and uncertainty. He cannot escape from the various responsibilities imposed upon him: Hari's sisters would have to marry, one day.

The search for job and a wish to escape such dark gloomy material condition lead Hari to Bombay where in the beginning we see him as a naïve startled boy struck with wonder and fear. But gradually along with a job he gains confidence, and like the mythical Ram, he comes back to his native village. He has defeated poverty, and has brought home money and plans for the future like the way Ram brought Sita. In the meantime, Lila with her bold and wise efforts has already helped her mother to regain health, and her father has already stopped drinking.

It is only in this novel that the wishes of the protagonists are fulfilled; in all the others they remain far beyond the reach or even understanding of the characters. The material concerns of day-to-day life get thematic significance only in this novel, and to some extent, in *In Custody*. In all the other novels Mrs. Desai's major preoccupations are with psychological and philosophical concerns.

Having given a detailed graphic picture of the characters of Anita Desai in the themes closely connected with postmodernism, it is in place to trace the postmodern elements in Anita Desai's fiction. The socio-cultural settings of her novels, dealt in detail in this chapter, call for a detailed study of the elements that make her a postmodernist writer.

NOTES

1. Anita Desai, *Fire on the Mountain* (Penguin, 1984), p. 132.
2. A.V. Krishna Rao, *Voices in the City, A Study: Perspectives on Anita Desai*, ed. Ramesh K. Srivastava (Ghaziabad: Vimal, 1984), p. 175.
3. Yashodhara Dalmia, "An Interview with Anita Desai," *The Times of India*, Sunday, April, 29, 1979, p. 13.
4. Darshan Singh Maini, "The Achievement of Anita Desai," in K.K. Sharma, ed., *Indo-Anglian Literature: A Collection of Critical Essays* (Ghaziabad: Vimal, 1977), p. 220.
5. Anita Desai, *Cry, the Peacock* (London: Peter Owen, 1963; Delhi, Orient Paperbacks, 1986), pp. 54-55.
6. Som P. Sharma and Kamal Awaste, "Anita Desai's *Cry, the Peacock*, A Vindication of the Feminine," in Ramesh Srivastava, p. 138.
7. R.S. Sharma, *Anita Desai* (New Delhi: Arnold Heinemann, 1981), p. 123.
8. Madhusudan Prasad, *Anita Desai: The Novelist* (Allahabad: New Horizon, 1981), p. 54.
9. Premila Paul and R. Padmanabhan Nair, "Varieties of Loneliness in *Fire on the Mountain*," in Indian *Women Writers*, ed. R.K. Dhawan (New Delhi: Prestige, 1991), Set I, Vol. III, p. 217.

10. Anita Desai, *In Custody* (London: William Heinemann, 1984), p. 113.
11. Anita Desai in "An Interview with Anita Desai," by Atma Ram, *World Literature Written in English*, Vol. 16, No. 1, April 1977, p. 100.
12. Ramesh K. Srivastava, "Anita Desai at Work: An Interview," in *Perspectives on Anita Desai*, pp. 224-25.

Chapter IV

The Postmodernist Scenario: A View of the World of Anita Desai

As stated earlier, the demarcation line between Modernism and Postmodernism becomes thinner as it is viewed within the Indian context. Indian English fiction offers this view remarkably well. This is evident in almost all the novels of Anita Desai. Her characters like Maya, Monisha, Nur, Bim, Tara and others inhabit the world which is modernist and postmodernist at the same time. Anita Desai's exploration of the female psyche which reveals the inner suffering of the women marks the modernist approach, whereas the fact that they are the entities worthy of this exploration, and it is being done by a woman herself raises the postmodernist issue. The span of time allocated to Postmodernism in the Western context is from 1960 to 1990. Its reverberations in the Indian context are felt even today as it happens in the case of several movements that come down from the West. Anita Desai's characters, women characters, in particular, offer a dualistic view of life combined with the past and the present.

Anita Desai's protagonists are highly sensitive and are desperate to seek liberation. This results in depicting realistic conformist and non-conformist types of women. Disillusioned, tortured and emotionally isolated, they find their survival threatened. Silence becomes their natural condition. As a woman writer, Anita Desai has added a new dimension in portraying women. N.R. Gopal writes:

> Anita Desai happens to be a leading voice. We may miss in her fiction the customary strains of rural poverty, caste and class conflicts, but she has fascinating stories to tell about individuals who have had to traverse a ground too tricky and treacherous to handle smoothly.[1]

Anita Desai has depicted feminine sensibility and feminine psyche rather than action as most Indian English novelists do. Maya in *Cry, the Peacock* has been taught repeatedly that women are vulnerable which indirectly prompts her into actions that appear feminine. Vulnerable or violent in their roles, Anita Desai depicts women of all ages.

At a critical moment when traditional and cultural values had almost become suspect with the collapse of modernism, very few writers seemed less likely to survive. With the impact of western materialism in the postwar society, and particularly, in the post-Independence India, the novels of Anita Desai attracted readers from the west and drew inspiring reviews and commentaries. Her novels brought major critical shifts exemplifying a postmodernist style of writing, with the critical insistences on post-colonialism, urbanization, consumerism and critical race studies, relevant in the current times. She retains a powerful hold on readers and critics alike for having initiated the critique on post-modernism through her novels.

Anita Desai makes an attempt to explore this submerged truth through the exploration of the psyche of her characters against her own vision of life, which is basically dark. While interpersonal relations are absurd, hardly able to give any emotional or spiritual sustenance; conforming to social routine means drudgery, loss of freedom and individuality, and all the vocations and avocations are monotonous and senseless—hardly worth pursuing; when the world is full of violence and destruction, death hovers dangerously over every ray of hope and meaning threatening destruction. An individual feels lonely and alienated in such a morbidly dark world. He is hopeless and full of despair, acutely conscious as he is of a sense of worthlessness and absurdity of all objects and patterns around him. Faith in God that could have provided some sustenance to this hopeless, dark world is not sought by Anita Desai's intellectual characters.

With nothing pleasant to live for, almost all her characters revolt against the existing patterns of life but as they do not have anything to fight for, their fight remains half-hearted and ends in failure. Sometimes instead of fighting they tend only to withdraw; but to their shock, they realize in time, that their attempts are futile because withdrawal is unattainable. If they try to seek relief in another world—the world of fantasy, after entering it they come to realize that it is no better than the world of reality. Thus man is entangled in a maze from which there is no way out. He writhes in pain all the time and waits for death which too is incapable of giving any meaning to his waiting. Though Desai basically seems to be saying—the longer one lives, the deeper he suffers the bitter assaults of existence, yet in her later novels, the change to a more positive attitude towards life is noticeable. This might have been the result of her own changing attitude to life, running almost parallel to her own growth and maturity.

In the novel *Clear Light of Day* it is in love that she sees the meaning and perfection of life. In *The Village by the Sea* she seems to be in favour of acceptance and adaptation to circumstances. In her novel *In Custody*, she seems to be advocating a welcome even to the calamities of life,

> The day would begin with its calamities. They would flash out of the sky and cut him down like swords. He would run to meet them. (204)

Life is still meaningless and man is continuously being assaulted by existence, yet it is better to face life boldly, to adapt oneself to it, and to make an effort to find some meaning in it. From this vision of life in Anita Desai's novels, begins the discourse of postmodernism whose main ingredients are interpersonal relations and alienation, obsession with death and violence, the deadly clutches of harsh reality, and impersonal forces like those of place and time. The interpersonal relations have been dealt in terms of husband-wife, parents-children, brothers-sisters and individual-society relations. Amongst these, the husband-wife relationship figures most prominently, but it is seldom harmonious or satisfying. All her female protagonists have a heightened physical and emotional sensitivity; while on the other hand, their male partners tend to be comparatively stolid, practical and matter-of-fact persons, hardly able to share or even appreciate of the world of their wives. This temperamental incompatibility naturally leads to alienation. Moreover, the female protagonists seem to value their individuality, privacy and freedom so much that they cannot bear to be possessed or suffer any encroachment on their world, even if it be by their husbands. Maya, Sita, Monisha, Amla, and Nanda—all of them want to be loved, but the love they desire is one that is pure and non-binding, one that is capable of giving freedom, not taking it. This is hardly possible because love in this world is invariably associated with duty, obligation, and loss of freedom and individuality.

Anita Desai has survived every successive wave of critical comments and observations regarding enormous transformations, colonization, socio-economic-cultural structures, and gender studies witnessed on the subcontinent of India. She invites our attention as one of the most rewarding novelists of the time. In doing so, Anita Desai has recorded the issues of modernism that were at stake. Her concerns constitute the arenas of individuals and family, the nation and the literary aspects—all of which make her a woman writer of great magnitude. Her preoccupation with odd, the other and alien woman through the exploration of the female psyche pins her as a literary critic with profound prescience. This reveals the postmodernist tendencies in her work, confirming the belief that modernism and postmodernism are not really at loggerheads each time.

In the dominant middle class, the loss of human relationships within the family has its effects on public and private lives. Any change affects the woman more. With this effect on woman a new kind of literary text emerged on the Indian soil. Anita Desai is considered the pioneer of psychological writing in Indian English field, as she poignantly portrays the changes in postmodern India and the deep impact they have had on the lives of women.

To understand the features of this new text, one has to understand the influences of the twentieth century on writers. It appeared that the entire gamut of women's writings had to be examined with great attention. The women writers focused on the image of woman in the expression of the subterranean and subconscious through history, culture, religion and psychology with a new perspective which added a new dimension to the writing called postmodern writing.

The Indian family which has been based on the institution of marriage grew out of the traditional patriarchal family grounded in the rhythms of agricultural production. As the economy shifted from domestic production to business, and to the industry with the impact of Industrial Revolution, a new kind of family life emerged with changes in religious cultural, economic organizations and in the mindset of the middle class woman.

Anita Desai created new trends in literary scene through the treatment of various themes relevant to the middle class Indian family: society, nation, women, seasons, cities, culture, and poetry, various approaches to religion, philosophy and psychology. With the Englishmen having left India, the dominant impetus of the writers shifted from national concerns to social issues and the needs of everyday life. Their successes or failures led to a sort of alienation from society. Their language was the language of loneliness—a postmodern development of thought and narration. The diehard followers of colonization lived in fantasizing the rich colonial past of "musical soirees" etc.

The postcolonial or postmodern writers expressed a sense of dissatisfaction with the repetitive themes of colonial sentimentalism. Also there was inaccessibility to this art form to reach common man due to the dissociation of art from entertainment. The postmodern artists strove to bridge this gap with large-scale assimilation of the popular or mass culture. The novels were filled with galleries of characters, crowded cities, shopping culture, education without values and emancipation of women.

The exploration of the psyche of women produced new and differing points of view and established new dimension of postmodern writing. With the focus on the problems of women, the literary strategies widely differed in the process of narrative self and the constructs of the text. There was a shift from the conventional plot and characters and the dimension of time and space. The meaning of the text was delusory, leading to the study of the self. This kind of decentering from the socio-cultural-economic-political sphere to the exploration of the self was the definitive form of postmodern novel. Postmodern literature is described as "apocalyptic" in the sense it dissolutes, the narrative self and the represented world.

A postmodernist protagonist is hopelessly sick and is unsure of his or herself to speak about the crisis. There is an absence of the psychological growth in these human figures of postmodern fiction which comes out as character's alienational experience. In *Cry, the Peacock*, Maya's explicit declaration reveals this state of the protagonist: "I am in fever, stop me . . . for I am ill. I am in a fever, God, in a fever."[2] The existence of the protagonist is "negative" to the cause or events and functions as a liquid capital to be extremely disposable. In other words, a postmodernist's novel is dehumanized.

Lured by materialism of the west, and with the loss of spiritual and traditional values, the postmodern educated young men and women were taking up jobs, adrift from parental homes—like Nirode and Amla in *Voices in the City*—with a quest for new values.

The images portray a dehumanization of characters and a spirit of melancholy in thoughts. In *Voices in the City* Nirode is wearied by his own uncertainty in which,

> He swept back and forth like a long weed undulating under water, a weed that could live only in aqueous gloom, would never rise and sprout into clear day light.[3]

The growing materialism and failing relationships created loneliness in human life in cities. Postmodern characters created by Anita Desai—Monisha and Nirode and Maya—reflect an emptiness of life which gives rise to unrest and dissociation of family ties. Joint families were turning to nuclear families in postmodern society. Clubs became decadent with raucous revelers, drunkards and dancers with an exhibition of masked violence.

The pursuit of money and luxury were an indispensable part of postmodern life. The process of urbanization precipitated through the literature of the moment has been best exemplified in Anita Desai's novels. The urban squalor, pursuit of characters for material prosperity and mundane pleasures create a sense of alienation. The cities present desolate, decayed and disintegrated pictures as Calcutta after monsoon or are repulsive and incomprehensibly cold like the houses and streets of London. "The houses and blocks of flats, streets and squares and crescents—the English habit of keeping all doors and windows tightly shut—of guarding their privacy" appear "a cold wasteland of brick and tile."[4] There is a clash between expectation and desire in postmodern situation. Monisha expects her husband to understand her and save her from the alleged theft highly attributed to her.

It is a prototype of postmodernity and the dichotomy in relationships: between the old and young, parent and child, husband and wife etc. These were becoming the major concerns challenging the very existence of relationships in both causes and effects. The scenario of postmodernism was different after the collapse of modernism: it influenced a pseudo life of the cities that was visible with its ugly guises of exploitation, emancipation, liberation with callousness, because of the decadent values and subsequent harsh realities. Though Indian women writers like Sarojini Naidu wrote about cuckoos and casuarinas, prominent writers like Mulk Raj Anand, Raja Rao and R.K. Narayan wrote mimetically about the social practices; the tragic theme of partition with its effects on women was frequently reflected in the works of Khushwant Singh and Anita Desai. Anita Desai in *Clear Light of Day* mentions:

> The city was in flames that summer. Every night fires lit up the horizon beyond the city walls so that sky was luridly tinted with festive flame of orange and pink, now and then, a column of white smoke would rise and stand solid as an obelisk in the dark.[5]

The romance of materialism today has inflated every angle of social, biological and individual aspirations. Women have become an important part of the change. According to Anita Desai, the loss of relationships between women and men immensely influenced the intricate negotiations of day-to-day life whose complex destinies dramatically heightened at every twist and turn. It is a bitter and harsh milieu from which the self craves to withdraw.

In an interview, Anita Desai mentions that she has been influenced by "European and American Literature."[6] Most of her men and women characters are maladjusted to the manners and attitudes that sculpt them as shipwrecked individuals, diverse from each other. Her novels reveal the author's deep concern with the upliftment of women. Anita Desai portrays different types of women. Maya is a married woman, Raka is a child, Nanda Kaul and Ila Das are old women. Maya is hypersensitive and a neurotic, Monisha is an intellectual type, Sarala (*In Custody*) cannot see beyond four walls of the house. All these women like to enjoy the love of men. They would have become different if the men had changed their attitudes towards them. Better understanding and correction of their aberration would have helped a great deal. It is Anita Desai's specific consideration that the gender conflicts were left unattended. It has been her life-long study to address this self-writing and gender-shaped society and its issues.

The postmodern women have a stress-ridden relationship with irresolvable problems with their husbands. They keep their ideas to themselves and have their own battles to fight and don't settle their scores clearly. It is not easy for them to flow with the current and stand by its "crest." The problem is that the women cannot flow and their heart cries as a result, they become the victims of the forces at play. The traditional image of a woman in the Indian context is perceived as a daughter, a wife and a mother. And if a woman does not fulfill any of these roles, a contradiction sets in. Maya and Monisha fail in their roles as wives. Motherhood becomes the ultimate objective and plays an important role in Desai's novels.

Maya withdraws after a long pining to accept her analytical and sublimely intellectual husband, Gautama, who has no interest in his wife's "insane passions." Maya's suicide becomes an enactment of her long-cherished desire for isolation and death. On the contrary, Monisha (*in Voices in the City*) commits suicide because of her simple-minded, non-entity of a husband, Jiban, who wants his wife "to be cheerful" to his people. He cannot understand her sensitivity to reading. However, by some "cultural logic" he admits his fault over Monisha's death.

As replicated, Maya and Monisha appear negative to the "cultural dominants" of the age and wish for release. Maya's unappeasable desire for simple physical fulfillment is created by culture. Women longing for love was something never represented in Indian English fiction; hence it gives this novel a postmodern edge. Besides, it opens another area of postmodern discussion where an unfulfilled woman seeks some kind of revenge. In short, Maya subconsciously desires her husband's death. She even passes a death verdict on Gautama, the man who had no contact with the world or with her. What would it matter to him if he died and lost even the possibility of contact? (*Cry*, 175)

Gautama's mixing of work and detachment in family life poses a difficulty for the reader in aesthetic terms. *Cry, the Peacock* is a conflict between an "analytic husband" and an "erotic wife" in Freudian terms. Trapped in a prisonhouse of desire, Maya becomes a neurotic after Gautama's death. In the postmodern milieu, Gautama's sister, Nila displaces desire to commodity acquisition. Maya's mother-in-law reveals a desire to understand the present culture as a product of the past culture, however nightmarish the past may be. She is a growth indicator to progressive thinking in the postmodern world. She does not take Maya to Calcutta due to her son's social and political obligations. She honours his present culture. Maya in her house of loneliness seeks to drown her erotic thoughts in the mundane materialism of her mother-in-law. The culturally backward society depicted by the novelist cannot be overlooked. Maya confesses:

> I can't . . . can't enter that silent darkened room where I shall have to be alone, gazing at the shadowed ceiling, the revolving fan with no one for company, not even a stray ray of light. (163)

Anita Desai represents the problems of women in the society that offers new possibilities as a part of postmodern situation. The postmodern narrative is an incomplete narration until we accept knowledge and power to represent the needs of women. Anita Desai's novels are studied for the psychological treatment of the women who are aware of their needs as women. She brings out the mental agony and unhindered processes of thoughts of her heroines and their disturbed mental states. N.R. Gopal points out:

> Anita Desai not only explores and portrays the feminine psyche of a common man but also of the subnormal bordering on abnormal women. These are the women who because of various factors are under so much of mental stress that they cannot be called insane but then certainly they are not normal. (122)

Accordingly, Anita Desai presents the concerns of married women in the postmodern culture. Maya is portrayed as an anti-heroine, a type of character one would never think of portraying in Indian English novels. The cultural acceptance of such women needs to be addressed in postmodern situation. Maya's cry is the cry of an agonized woman who contests to stand alone without taking refuge in art or spiritual solemnity. Hence she is broken.

Voices in the City explores the voices that are caught in the cross-currents of the changing social values of Calcutta. It is a new kind of reflex that the voices are examined in postmodern narration. Ramesh Srivastava writes: "It is not only in the subject matter, characterization and in presenting the atmosphere of mind but also in the use of narrative technique, symbols, images and the disturbed time-scheme that Anita Desai deserves to be called a psychological novelist." The novel shows a total rupturing of the cause and the events upon which the character, plot, novel's space and time depend, and introduces "alien forms and information."

Calcutta, with its squalor and futility and emptied out of its spiritual values, is portrayed through the pages of the novel like Eliot's Wasteland. Dust-covered city signifies the meaningless glitter, restlessness and fatigue of its inhabitants. The vast crowds, the gloom, the darkness, the decayed houses and streets inundated with water during monsoons are symptoms of the failure of human civilization.

The characters are intensely in search of peace and permanence in order to overcome their restlessness. They are different from conventional heroes and heroines and are limited in experience in their pursuit of life's meaning. Their failures are like the tragedy of Hamlet. The three protagonists, Monisha, Nirode and Amla are psychologically and physically alienated. Their personalities and attitudes determine their isolation. They lack the ability to establish social contacts. Monishà's suffering is not her creation, but is caused due to the lack of sensibility of her in-laws. There is a discursive brooding of self when Monisha looks at the women behind the barred windows waiting for their husbands.

> Lives spent in waiting for nothing waiting on men self-centered and indifferent and hungry and demanding and critical waiting for death and dying misunderstood always behind bars, those terrifying black bars that shut . . . in the old house, in the old city. (120)

The characters are intensely in search of peace and permanence in order to overcome their restlessness. They are different from conventional heroes and heroines and are limited in experience in their pursuit of life's meaning.

The historical feature of these women is a mute struggle for freedom and identity. It is their feminist need that is undermined and needs to be examined. Anita Desai's concern is that this gender captivity is a colonial legacy of pre-Independence India found even in our evolved society. She portrays these vices as they live and see through modern artificial world. To Monisha, the city of Calcutta neither offers respect nor privacy.

In postmodern art, the visual images of birds, cages and scorching summers are like traps that offer no solace from suffering, internally or externally, constructing them, as if by right, out of existence.

Monisha is trapped by every situation that happens to her when her in-laws misinterpret and manipulate her as if she were a liar; she suffers for not having a child—she can't bear the gossip and discussion on blocked fallopian tubes in an age of science and technology. As Shanta Krishnaswamy points out: "Being a woman is problem. All the rules and restrictions against which little girls chafed and women grumbled about were designed only to block all routes to escape from the conventional mode of living, from society that beastly tamer."

The strolling musicians depict the ugly decadent voices of the city. It shows how the institution of family has ruptured all relations between street life and private life. Postmodernism condemns the families being reduced to street shows with no ethical values.

If Nirode is the male version of Monisha in his wish for release from the trapped city, this suffering is distinctly the cry for identity as a writer. He is reduced to a "barricade of words," by the overriding editors and journalists of the day. Nirode's problem is his poor journalistic post, where writers are robbed of their ideas until they are established by the powerful hands of press. Unlike Gautama, Nirode understands his sister Monisha. On the contrary, Adit in *Bye, Bye Blackbird* is insensitive to the sufferings of Sarah. Similarly Raman fails to understand Sita in *Where Shall We Go This Summer?* An insensitive and brutal character, Preet Singh in *Fire on the Mountain* rapes and kills Ila Das.

Amla literalizes her relation to art to eke a capitalist value out of it. The monsoon wetness of rain is a disorienting factor to the people of Calcutta. The poor and rich are alike and desire death to overcome disappointment in life. The denizens of Calcutta are defined by Anita Desai:

> They share one face, one expression of tiredness, such overwhelming tiredness that even bitterness is merely passive and hopelessness makes the hand extend only feeble, then drop back without disappointment. (117)

Aunt Lila interprets the generation of Monisha as the diseased young generation. Her voice is free and fearless. It is her belief that their generation had won freedom for the nation and it was for the younger generation to achieve something beyond. But the unusual brooding of Monisha and Nirode is repudiation of the conventionalism of life, family and society. Anita Desai weaves the themes of emptiness, futility and death of talent—all this is reflected in *Voices in the City*. The overlapping silence against the bare rooms and squares of empty spaces rob life of all vitality and zest of creative talent. Amla is haunted by Monisha's head prodding out silently like a "stuffed rag doll." This—a shockingly arresting image of postmodern woman—is a kind of emotional anticlimax to death.

Anita Desai explores a variety of new and thought-provoking ways of illustrating the futility and existential predicament of postmodern Indian upper middle class women.

Mrs. Major Chadha is like a character from a Greek tragedy whose deliberate and suspended entry at the death of Monisha fills us with a severe contempt. Hers is a "faithless human arm" who keeps out from the failures of family to seek her own privacy among the hills in Kalimpong. To Nirode and Amla she appears as a fearful aura inspiring goddess Kali, who would pour blood "in birth" or "drain" it out "in death." Moving towards death, *Voices* refers to the evil nature of the spirit of the city "basically bloodthirsty Calcutta," "the Devil City," "the Monster

City," "the City of Death," "the City of Kali," "Goddess of Death," and as such the symbol of death is woven into the story. frustration, rootlessness, hopelessness, longing for death as an escape from the tensions of life.

According to Anita Desai, "Life is reality you see on the surface—the visible world while literature plunges the depths below that lie hidden and need to be explored and described."[6]

The most striking feature about 20th century Indian writing in English is that the romantic view of life and art has turned into an expression of self as a literary ideal. It is the expression of the suffering mind. Futility of existence is perceived as a disturbing truth. The impressions and experiences of these suffering minds combine in peculiar and unexpected ways to build up a rich pattern of meaning.

Bye, Bye Blackbird underlines the problem of racial discrimination of Indian immigrants who are marginalized in an alien culture. The characters are in a mystical search for "a still centre," a land of their lives. Dev is the blackbird who is not accepted into the English society—Mrs. Roscommon James is unsympathetic to accept a coloured Indian into English society. This is an outrageous insult to an Indian. Anita Desai is trying to convey that there can never be a unification of the Indian and western cultures; or even if there is, it is only a superficial one. There can be no true relation, only loneliness is possible in such an amalgamation. Sarah, a woman of English origin, marries Adit, an Indian. Sarah loses her identity and experiences an inexpressible conflict over her inconsiderate husband. Dev, another Indian, finds London uncomfortable, where people live in hiding. He finds them indifferent and insecure in their relationships and believes that they make relationships only when it is essential. The assaulted prejudice and the non-conformity of the English society towards the coloured Indians are often hovered on the brink of irresponsible attiude of the English. Further, the lack of suitable jobs for Indian immigrants or English people's objection to the gross behaviour of Indians in public life shows maladjustment of free Indians in the western world against the lost imperialists' attitude towards Indians.

Bye, Bye Blackbird is neither a psychological novel, nor does it deal with an explication of a personal problem. It is a reflection of the confusion of the values in the intermingling of the Indian and Western cultures. The novel gravitates from self to society and from societal condition to self where such contests are common to modern world. Adit's glamour for the English countryside and serenity is a fleeting gesture of appeal and frustration in response to his emotional need. Dev's condition is not different from this.

Sarah is another "stuffed rag doll" like Monisha, who ceaselessly searches for her identity through her changing roles in life. She plays so many diverse roles that, in the process, she loses herself. She experiences personal loss as a consequence of her marriage to an Indian. The harsh reality is: whether the character is Sarah or Maya or Monisha or Sita, an Indian woman loses her identity at birth itself. She is the daughter of a father, wife of a husband or mother of a son—that is all; she is never her "self." It is this social reward that a woman has earned over the generations in a man-made and man-dominated society. Now, this is a typical postmodern situation. The awareness of women about their pathetic condition is a result of the postmodernist factors that produced 'new' culture. This new culture consists of women's education, individual values attributed to them as independent entitles their hopes and aspirations and the final realization that they still are at the mercy of the 'system' which is unwilling to change. Postmodernism initiates debate on several issues including women's question and opens up new avenues of self-realization and achievement. Women in the west have achieved it to a considerable extent; Indian women are in the process of doing so

Meeṇakshi Mukherjee points out that "Sarah Sen" is a typical character of Anita Desai.[7] She is hypersensitive to the torrid "oriental heat" and "ugliness" of India. Sarah and Adit experience emptiness, a kind of melancholy in the "glamour less" India. They are tossed by the flood like "flotsam" and then become a part of it, "the black flood." Caught in the complexity of alienated cultures, Sarah suffers from loneliness. The expatriate Indian is an exile. The writer depicts this existential crisis of maladjustment, rootlessness and alienation that infest Dev, Adit and Sarah. Sarah's progress from Ms. Sarah to Mrs. Sarah Sen and Sarah the Head's Secretary sending out bills and taking in cheques makes her wonder if she had "any existence" of her own. She feels a "nobody" in an "absurd drama." Staring out of the window at the chimney pots and the clouds, she wondered: if [she] Sarah had any existence at all. Comparatively Adit's inner loneliness spills to the surface. Adit, the marginalized blackbird, discovers his roots and leaves England for India.

Though Art makes a closure to such an inequality of races in human society, reality presents directly the structure of class and its marginalized individuals, particularly woman.

Where Shall We Go This Summer? is a study of women in conflict. Sita's inability to live with her husband and her children is an existential predicament. Her obsession to escape to Manori islands is a cross-referencing to Maya's fantasizing her childhood days. Sita's longing to go back to Manori islands stems from the loss of interpersonal relationships and maladjustment with her husband, Raman. Her husband's lack of sensitivity drives her almost to insanity. Sita's marriage to Raman and movement to Bombay leave her disappointed. She discovers that "life is a mass of disillusionment and despair like the monsoon. The monsoon continued like an increasing burial. There was nothing to do with it but watch it, listen to it, sighing out of the window." (38) The monsoon is symbolic of human types and attitudes. Encountering an unnatural culture shock, Sita, a mother of four children, abandons her responsibility towards her family and turns into a woman of "rage," "fear" and "revolt." Sita is an exact opposite of the mythic Sita. Her moving away from the traditional image is the ugly dimension of emancipation: "People to Sita are nothing—nothing but appetite and sex. Only food, sex and money matter. Animals." (14) Sita does not like the "vegetarian complacency," the "subhuman plaudity" and "sluggishness" of the people. The stereotype life of cooking and procreating provokes her to revolt. She smokes to get a relish of her life only to find that islanders too were not free from cruelty and violence. She cannot live for long as her children accuse her of such a transgression of her duty. Sita symbolically represents the lost values of modern wasteland. By an intellectual irony, she returns to Bombay. Unlike the other women protagonists, Sita does not end her life or turn into a neurotic but accepts defeat and her duty to her family, which is the inescapable chagrin of a woman in a man-made society. Sita's reaction raises the basic question about the possibility and limitations of a woman. It is that the woman's position is irredeemable that makes the novel, *Where Shall We Go This Summer?* unique among the themes concerned with postmodern issues.

In Anita Desai's next novel *Fire on the Mountain*, Nanda Kaul is pitted against the familial duties by her people as if it were their right. Nanda Kaul retires to the secluded Carignano, in Kasauli, Simla. The novel connects the existentialist concerns and familial obligations of the upper middle class women. Nanda Kaul's predicament is her healthy and protected life which becomes a relentless bondage to social inequality. It is her "failure" that her children are "alien to her nature." Nanda Kaul has discharged her duties at such time of her life that she wanted to live without attachments. She disapproves of the torture of "demands" and "requests" of her family, who remember her only for the selfish reasons. Nanda Kaul has no feeling for them and wants to be immune like the "wooden hills." She is irritated with her daughter Asha's messing up with Tara's life and consequently Raka, the helpless great grand-daughter who is in need of recuperation after illness.

Nanda Kaul feels that she has enjoyed nothing to be subjected to such a fatality. Her Vice-Chancellor husband Mr. Kaul, shared a secret love with Ms. David all his life. Her children betrayed her. It is the indifference of her husband and her children that infuriates her to be bonded once again to the cycle of duties and obligations. Nanda Kaul feels vulnerable and cut off. Her actions are defensive and calculated to protect her interests. Anita Desai tries to introduce the alienation of the children as a consequence of the failure of woman as a mother. Society's success or failure lies in woman, the centre of social construct. Perhaps only woman is to blame for her failure and not the society, for exploitation is the contention of postmodern thinkers who are out to subvert the conventional norms.

In a way she approves of Raka because of the girl's love to be left alone. Raka shows Nanda Kaul's sensitivity in her search for freedom away from the life of city. The little girl has seen the harsh realities—the cruelty of her father beating her mother and embittered childhood. As a result, the girl suffers from an unnatural fear of cruelty and insecurity. The forest fire on the mountain distresses her sleep, lest it might creep and catch her unawares. It is this kind of a "dream-disaster" full of "spectres" that haunt one after the other like a trap. Like Nanda Kaul she keeps awake to see if the fires stopped. To Nanda Kaul, the fire or the effect of the impending storm constitutes a potential calamity to life, like the unexpected request from Asha. It makes her life bitter. Nanda Kaul does not resist the bitterness but swallows it, bears it by telling fairytales, stories of her father in Tibet which are full of lies to captivate Raka. Her belief is that life is built "on lies" and nobody wants "truth" because nobody can "stand it." If Nanda Kaul gives descriptive articulation to evade reality to Raka, Anita Desai portrays her as a simplified "subaltern voice" who is disposed by her family.

Fire on the Mountain points the agonizing shameful condition of women in the society through different characters like Nanda Kaul, Asha, Ila Das and Raka—all of whom are rejected and suffer in one way or the other at the hands of the men.

Ila Das tries to save Preet Singh's daughter from the cruelty of being sold to a rich landowner, but becomes a victim of it herself. It is the generic helplessness of woman to save her life and honour from the cruelty of man, is Anita Desai's motif. The title *Fire on the Mountain* symbolically depicts the cruelty and violence prevalent in the male-dominated society. Ila Das and Nanda Kaul develop a kind of resignation to life and its "rigmarole" of duties and obligation. It is this tired and exhausted woman who distrusts anything new that makes the book a postmodern novel.

Fire on the Mountain—though it conveys the helplessness of women—shows an incipient mode of preparedness of these women to lead life independently by a kind of constructive intuition and introspection. That women like Nanda Kaul were resisting metropolitan life style to adopt new modes of thought and life is manifest throughout. Anita Desai defines that the real meaning of life is the beginning of freedom of expression of women which is postmodern trend of thinking.

Anita Desai's contribution to the psychological novel has been influenced by Virginia Woolf and Camus. She prepares the Indian psyche to elements like alienation and loneliness. Some critics have cited that Anita Desai joins the female authors like George Eliot, Virginia Woolf, and Jane Austen whose heroines continuously fight for their rights and assert their individuality.

> I have been reading Virginia Woolf and Camus since my student days with the greatest admiration and interest. They have certainly influenced me tremendously.

In *Clear Light of the Day* Time is presented as the fourth dimension of human existence. Time moves back and forth, Anita Desai connects them by depicting that Time as destroyer and the preserver, the flux and reflex of consciousness where past, present and future mixed together. The action of the story is unfolded through flashback childhood memories of Tara and Bim. Tara and Bim are contrasted in their life styles as well as in their natures. To Anita Desai, the centre of the fictional construct becomes some dominant consciousness.

On visiting her parents' home in Delhi, Tara is upset to see her brother and sister like the antiques unchanged with time. She attempts to bring her brother, Baba out of his cocoon. Ironically, she lives a hollow life with her husband, Bakul, who only graces his house and parties. Tara's recollections of her childhood days are joyless memories, her father "pressing syringes" into her mother's arm or the "muddy trickle" of the river Jumna which contains the "ashes" of her aunt etc. Tara suffered from fear and insecurity during her adolescence, when her brother Raja departed to Hyderabad refusing to share the family responsibility. The memories of Aunt Mira's ill-treatment by her in-laws develop a kind of anti-marriage attitude in Tara. If partition brought social and cultural barriers between people, the growing consciousness and search for individuality is the central conflict between Tara and Bim.

On the other hand Bim develops a feeling of kindness on looking back at Tara and Raja of having conspired to be cruel and unkind to her, or her brother turning into a landlord and buying her house. She realizes that her stubborn nature had blinded her from understanding the true feelings of Tara and Raja to start a new route of life.

If Tara feels her presence harsh and disturbing, and her superiority complex and petrifying harshness towards Baba, Bim analyzes her reason for being harsh and determines to clean her "dirty mind." Though realization and penitence is the beginning of the clarity of her mind, she fears the task of "reconciliation" and "forgiveness." Her feminine self feels an unfathomable love scare for her sister and her brother by the "clear light of the day." (165) Unmarried and opting for the life of a spinster she reflects Anita Desai's vision of the identity of the new Indian woman. From hatred to love, from alienation to accommodation, Bim truly moves towards a genuine and authentic identity. Her emotional callousness, silence, nevertheless, end in a positive note. Ultimately all opposing notes mingle and meet at the roots.

The birthday party of Mulk's Guru enables Bim to see how time affects human life. Guru's aged voice is "plagued" by time and Mulk's "innocent" and "youthful" voice is untouched by Time, like the love in T.S. Eliot's *Four Quartets:* "Time the destroyer is time the preserver." (162) It is time that brings about change in the lives of the characters in the novel.

Bim's growth of self makes her understand Aunt Mira's right to live a normal life and her searing pangs of widowed existence. The death of the cow generates further isolation to Aunt Mira. It draws her into a fierce trap of death by suicide. The incidents add to the textural density of alienation and render a new dimension to Bim's personal identity. Bim comprehends the true meaning of life. It is love, the clear light of the day that gives human life, light and meaning. If Nanda Kaul and Ila Das (*Fire on the Mountain*) have been loveless and were clogged in the machine of life, Bim is ennobled with love, love which dispels the chaos, confusion, complexes, depression and despair. From lovelessness of Nanda Kaul to love in Bim progresses to a human and natural identity. From escape of responsibilities to acceptance of responsibilities is the ennobling experience of love. Love is ennobling. But to be bound by guardianship is accentuated in *In Custody*.

Unlike other novels, the protagonist in *In Custody* is Deven, a male. Sarla, Deven's wife, is frustrated over her husband's economic inability as a temporary lecturer at Lila Ram Lal College, Mirpore. Although Deven and Sarla understand the secret about each other, it does not bring up any closeness of spirit and comradeship. It is the complexities and disappointments that dense their lives. At least Deven had his poetry to take refuge; Sarla has nothing and is filled with "accusation" and "bitterness." It is Nur's outburst on his marriage to two loveless women that makes Deven see the similarity in his own life.

For Imtiaz Begum, Nur's second wife, art should be a means of livelihood. To Murad, Deven and Nur, art requires a total, "selfless dedication." Though Mr. Abid Siddiqui, Head of Urdu Department persuades the college authorities to fund the project of recording Nur's poetry after the initial failure, Deven does not succeed. In a different way but with the same attitude, the first wife of Nur offers to help Deven if he makes some "payment" "for the provision." Deven realizes he is trapped; so also is Nur who is trapped between his wives. This is locally the practical problem of whatever class or strata one belongs to, there is no escape from the necessity of earning one's livelihood. Human beings are trapped by relationships and restrictions that obstruct an ordinary man or poet. The desire to escape from this burden is beset with insecurity and inadequacy.

Nur is a great poet but leads an undisciplined life of wine and women, fools and idlers to quizzically accentuate Nur's drunkenness, neglectful and a complaining and ill-tempered person. Deven's dream mission is shattered when he begins to see the basic nature of life and its workings. Deven's lack of professional competence and technical skill and his passion for Urdu poetry (an unconscious desire to serve his father's love for Urdu poetry) are darkened with depravity and hopelessness. This is a postmodern conflict of passion and restrictions. It seems to Deven as if Murad, Siddique and Nur's wives have caged him. Nur realizes that he is the victim of other people and situations. A victim marginalized not only by others but also by his own doubts and dullness.

In a world where human nature and "evils of technology" are at constant play, the pursuit of immortality of art is a postmodern challenge. Deven always fantasized that poetry is man's dream world and the ideal not real.

If the dream becomes the reality of life it will not be like the dream and if dreams are not ideal but real, "then the bubble would be breached and burst and it would no longer be perfect. And if it were not perfect, and constant, then it would all have been for nothing, it would be nothing." (192) Deven with the fantasy of the poet being shattered intends to keep Nur's poetry and poetic genius alive even after his death. He is now forced to accept Nur's life as another facet of reality. In doing so he would become Nur's custodian as a resolution of his inner drama. He emerges into a new self with a regenerated spirit. Anita Desai brings out the irony of custody: custody means guardianship, safe-keeping as well as imprisonment. (194)

In the postmodern idiom, art and artiste are fused. Deven learns to accept through Nur's life that art and artist are inextricably woven and committed to each other. The commitment to art is the postmodern resolve to the metaphor of the title, *In Custody*. The conflict-ridden Deven evolves as an intellectually engaging and coping with life with greater joy than ever.

Baumgartner's Bombay traces the story of a German Jew who escapes the horrors of Nazi war under compelling conditions, arrives in India to undertake some business for livelihood. He remains an outsider with an existential dilemma to happiness and love. Exiled from happiness and love, his life is adrift with untold fears, agonies and miseries that make him a schizophrenic. In British India, he experiences a peculiar kind of defeat and helplessness whether he deserved it or not. Captured by the British and bullied by his own countrymen (Germans) he finds no resolution to crisis. He ironically represents the post-war, post-famine Calcutta which is on the verge of tragic partition. In such a situation his existence is absurd and he is condemned to the life of an exile. This was how the world ended, there was no other ending.

His end comes suddenly from a German Aryan who detests Baumgartner from the beginning. Though Baumgartner has changed his attitude after living in India for the last fifty years, his colonial thinking makes him an outsider and creates disturbing problems. He is caught in an existential dilemma.

Lotte's choice of her life makes her an appallingly unbearable woman where men are centralized, marginalizing such women into a non-existential zone of living. "In patriarchal society, women are split subjects who watch themselves being watched by men. They turn themselves into object because femininity itself is defined by being gazed upon by men." Victims of God, or nature or society or man, Anita Desai's novels are expressions of marginalized beings whose experiences become the focus of attention and primary concern of the novelist. Baumgartner's Bombay is a representative postmodernist text. The protagonist, and alienated being who has migrated to India, is haunted by fear and self-pity. The world around him is alien, and though the result of his own choice, the self-exile haunts him continuously. He distrusts those who love him and is unable to make out friends from foes. This peculiar state of mind which is close to paranoia is a result of migration, cultural duality and commingling of international boundaries. A German Jew, brought to India by the circumstances, successfully overcomes the outer issues like obtaining Indian citizenship. Baumgartner, however, is caught within his own mental disorder. The situation, resembling the modernist dilemma, is in fact, the postmodernist problem. Anita Desai's characters are pitted against unfavourable socio-cultural circumstances which represent several issues of contemporaneity, and the characters emerge as the product of postmodern situation. The crisis of identity becomes a major issue with Anita Desai as a novelist. *In Bye-Bye Blackbird*, the protagonist faces the dilemma of finding his place in the society. Maya in *Cry, the Peacock,* Tara in *Clear Light of the Day*, Nirode in *Voices in the City* and the protagonist in *Baumgartner's Bombay* are caught in more or less a similar situation. They are the victims of contemporary socio-cultural factors which together can be termed as postmodern. Thus Anita Desai's women revolt against injustice, revolt at a human level or resign due to hypersensitivity. They confront a kind of psychic truth different from reality. Anita Desai's women are driven into themselves to realize their own self. In the process they develop fears, obsessions, neurosis, and schizophrenia and gradually withdraw from society including families and husbands. The incommunication and aloofness of these women is what connects Desai's novels and makes her an exceptionally unique novelist.

To deal with so many intricate problems of postmodern lives of men and women, Anita Desai required powerful techniques of narration. An analysis of her narrative techniques would help the critic realize that in both content and structure Anita Desai proved herself a superior artist to her contemporary writers.

NOTES

1. N.R. Gopal, *A Critical Study of the Novels of Anita Desai* (Atlantic, New Delhi, 1995), p. 2.
2. Anita Desai, *Cry the Peacock* (Delhi: Orient, 1980), p. 18.
3. Anita Desai, Voices in the City (New Delhi: Orient Paperbacks, 1982), 63-64. Anita Desai, *Bye, Bye, Blackbird* (New Delhi: Hind Pocket Books, 1971, p. 70.
4. Anita Desai, *Clear Light of Day* (New Delhi: Allied, 1980), p. 44.
5. Ramesh K. Srivastava, *Perspectives on Anita Desai* (Ghaziabad: Vimal, 1984), p. 210.

Chapter V

The Narrative Technique: Postmodernist Mode of Expression

To a postmodern writer the language of communication is the resulting expression of the characters, their emotions, their sentiments etc. Language is a means to display the reality i.e., the drab incidents that exist in human life. The purpose of the writer is to convey the truth or to discover one's self in writing. Apart from a powerful communicative language, the postmodern writer also uses narrative techniques to portray the boredom of life in a very interesting style.

In a postmodern context, the creation of characters is a cultural construct. Any cultural construct of character will privilege meanings and experience to some, or de-privilege others. In other words, the postmodern narrators attempt to show the mood and the mind, the will and the turmoil of the characters. They examine the 'cracks,' the 'silences,' the discontinuities carried by the characters, and deconstruct or demystify the cultural meanings that surround them. In an identifiable way, they reveal the meaning about the reality of the character beyond the rhetorical construct.

Anita Desai's admission of her style and writing is an effort to discover, underline and convey the significance of things.[1] The significance of Anita Desai's novels lies in her narrations. Influenced by writers like James Joyce, Virginia Woolf, Albert Camus, who are regarded as the masters of modernist art, Mrs. Desai uses their modes of expression for the postmodernist purpose. She uses her narrative techniques to initiate the discourse of postmodernism to describe a particular consciousness. Shifting the realm of writing as a social instrument to the study of the nocturnal mind, Desai's novels convey a perennial interest in human relationships like those "through blood and marriage."[2]

Anita Desai's novels are qualitatively different from those of her contemporary writers. The novels talk about her craft of writing. Equally consumed by a popular audience for mere entertainment and as a postmodern objective to bridge the art and craft of writing, they offer tremendous potential for research scholarship. Anita Desai is a balanced writer with artistic greatness and critical insights to create a genre of postmodern narration. Though her narrative techniques appear to have been borrowed from European writers, she uses them, most creatively to portray her theme close to reality. An attempt to study her fictional apparatus, gives an anatomy of her novels. The aim of this chapter is to identify and classify the narrative strategies and techniques of Anita Desai which she uses in the pursuit of her literary objectives to explicate concepts like love, truth, understanding and harmony. Anita Desai's muse and inspiration, life and experience as focused and observed in her novels is the search for the true meaning of life where the imprisoned "voices" of her women cry for life and love.

Anita Desai's technique of narration discourses on Indian culture, history, social structure, religion and psychology in order to define the meaning of life. With the influence of the western writers, there was a compelling need to relate between the cultural moments. Anita Desai uses techniques like voices of the characters, point of view, letters, time, stream of consciousness and culture, flashbacks, contrast, introspection, quotes from diverse poets, symbolism and imagery, multiple narrators, Indian ness, irony, rhetoric, childhood as the field where the future attitudes are sown, continuous and discontinuous discourses and artificial culture touched by vulgarity. Although all these modes do not conform to the postmodernist technique alone, they nevertheless, steer the narration out of the modernist cliché, and assume the turn of a new contemporary narration.

The technique of Anita Desai defines the meaning of the novel by multiple and heterogeneous social voices. Such a technique may be disconnected in time and space in the development of the story; but contribute "textually" and "intertextually" to her larger meaning of life as in *Voices in the City*. The multiple narrators, Nirode, Monisha and Amla are in search of a meaning of their life. A major fictional technique that Anita Desai introduces is an intertextuality of narration. Henry James' statement about the technique: "Life [is] all inclusion and confusion and art [is] all discrimination and selection."[3]

The story of *Clear Light of Day* is narrated from Bim's point of view; she is the protagonist and the voice of the author. Anita Desai uses diverse techniques like these which give new expression to the complex stratifications of her character and new meaning to her works.

Anita Desai uses even a letter as a technique to hint the postmodern debate on the unrealized potential of women. To achieve this, she effectively changes her language from diction to discourse. For example, in *In Custody* the language used at places indicates the ideological discourse of a woman writer:

> Are you not guilty of assuming that because you are a male, you have right to brains, talent, reputation and achievement, while I, because I was born female am condemned to find what satisfaction I can in being maligned, mocked, ignored and neglected? Is it not you who has made the play the role of the loose woman in gandy garments by refusing to take my work seriously and giving me just that much regard as the artist was made? In this unfair world that you have created what else could I have been but what I am? Ask yourself that when you peruse my verses, if you have the courage. (196)

Anita Desai is hinting to Deven that dismissal of women is dismissal of art which would be a postmodern conjunction to the neglect of women. This single letter has the potential to open up a long debate on women in postcolonial India.

Another potent technique of Anita Desai is flashback. She develops the subject of the growth of the self through the contrasting consciousness of Tara and Bim. The flashback memories and experiences of these characters unfold the action of the entire tale. The contrasting consciousness of Tara and Bim and the "time" in which they are placed become techniques in the writer's hand to portray the experiences of these two characters. Bim is preoccupied with family responsibilities and has no time for introspection. Anita Desai draws a contrast in the characters of Tara and Bim. Tara carries hurtful thoughts of Raja, like stings of bee and suffers from them due to lack of courage. She does not give herself a chance to be treated and as a result remains deeply affected for the rest of her life. She even avoids the company of Raja and Bim not to be wounded again. She fails to grow as she doesn't perceive any meaning in her life. On the other hand, initially Bim misunderstands Tara and Raja, and is disturbed deeply with the mishappening of Aunt Mira. She temporarily experiences a sense of fear and insecurity; but changes into a wiser and nobler being with the passage of time. Time changes her and with an epiphanic transformation she gives up her mental conflict over her sister and brothers.

This is the growth of Bim's self which recognizes that her mind moved from past time to present time to see clearly internally and externally and welcome life in the clear light of day with love. If relationship is what matters, Anita Desai uses the dimension of time as the source of continuity and an inescapable character. Time, in a typical Shelleyian mode, is the preserver, destroyer and creator. If Time healed Bim to an ennobled self, it stopped movement with Tara. Yet, Time preserved Mulk's youthful voice like a child with a touch of sweetness, whereas Time "cracked" "to break" the voice of Mulk's Guru. This movement in and out of Time evokes the Postmodernist writer's concern for reality which takes him back to the past, and into the future, finally making him realize the significance of the present.

The fictional technique used in *Bye-Bye Blackbird* is the depiction of contrast of opinions and attitudes. Adit, Dev and Sarah are like three different cups trying to establish their individuality on a foreign soil. The racial alienation is at conflict and the protagonists seek compromise and conciliation. Their 'cry' is at injustice and social acceptance. Everything that Desai conveys about the conflict is to forge a new identity and towards the acceptance of expatriate sensibility. This contrast of opinions represents the situation after migration into a foreign land where conflict with the native is inevitable. It results into alienation which is a postmodern social trend in contemporary society.

Adit, an Indian settled in London, marries Sarah, an English woman and Dev an Indian who is not so enchanted with London goes to London for study. The contrast is ironically comic. Dev who had been brought up on in English literature and English culture in India through the pages of Dickens and Lamb, Addison and Boswell, cannot recognize the original around him and within his reach.

The situation becomes doubly ironic when Dev—responding to an advertisement—discovers that the prospective employer wanting to expand business in India is not a Britisher but an Indian:

> The smooth Oxbridge accents that had slid down the telephone wires earlier that morning had led him to expect someone sleek, pink and British, an adventurous city man seeking to extend his empire to the fabled India of silks and tigers' skin. Instead, here was a young India of distinctly Dravidian complexion dressed ostentatiously. (28)

So is also Krishna Swami in for an ironic surprise when he sees Dev.

Adit cannot beget mature love. He is only a "potted plant" struggling to grow in English soil with no natural air or food. It is a symbolic fact that an exile is an exile everywhere. The struggle for equal status with Englishmen is only a dream. Further the differences encountered like the academic life of London, the unacceptable nature of Englishmen, their blighting insults at Indians suggest the gap between Indian and English cultures that cannot mutually reconcile with each other.

Time brings change, isolation, disconnectedness, death in the world of Anita Desai' novels. The characters move forward and backward in time. Time establishes the connection between character and narration. Monisha views the past and present as two different "ghosts" meeting face to face, and thinks of the past as history which lingers like "a long twilight." It cloys Monisha and she finds that its essence lingers everywhere." It is one passage of time moving from one "date to another," where she cannot understand to what "purpose," what "history" and what "time" it leads to.

Time and history are a collective consciousness in Desai's novels. It is time which connects the individual and the event. To Desai, the past and present are never separate or are not strangers but are lost to be configurated. Where the past stops and where the present begins are like cubist compositions to Desai.

The use of brilliant couplets in Urdu over the death of a pet dog in *Cry, the Peacock*—the juxtaposition of the serious and the light-hearted—is a device used by a postmodernist novelist. When Maya laments the death of her pet dog, Toto, Gautama quotes softly an Urdu couplet:

> Even if each star in the sky were an heart, what of it? Give me one heart that is capable of sorrow. (22-23)

Anita Desai uses Gautama's passionate objectivism, on a poetic level as a consolation to Maya's cry for physical fulfillment. Later, when Maya is caught in the fear of death that she might die without enjoying the ecstasy of being alive, a gentle voice consoles Maya from inside:

> Lord, thou hast dealt me so many sorrows, to bear them; couldst thou not also have lent me another heart? (103)

Surely it was a door welcoming her to bear. Like her characters, Anita Desai searches for meaning from within. Anita Desai uses rhetorical expressions to reinforce the theme of the novel. Maya cries to save herself. "Father! Brother! Husband! Who is saviour? I am in need of one. I am dying, and I am in love with living. I am in love and I am dying." (98)

When Maya wishes to be outside with Gautama, Gautama discourses to Maya on life attached to sense objects in order to indoctrinate a life of detachment:

> Thinking of sense objects, man becomes attached thereto. From attachment arises longing and from longing anger is born. From anger rises delusion; from delusion, loss of memory is caused. From loss of memory the discriminative faculty is ruined and from the ruin of discrimination, he perishes. (112)

Indeed the ideology of Raisahab is "to accept" works upon Maya's consciousness until she is cleansed of the black magic. R.S. Sharma rightly points out: "Most of her (Desai's) problems as a fiction writer begin with her insistence on too much style on too small a canvas."[4] However, a free intelligibility of conversation and high strung sensitiveness add flavour to Anita Desai's style.

The customs and culture are potently used to portray the reality and bring out the essence of the characters. If Maya is obsessed with the childhood prophecy, she exhibits a radicalized consciousness of modernity, with no botheration of custom and tradition:

> Logic, tact, diplomacy—nothing to her who chattered so glibly and gaily all the day by, jumping up now and then to bring out a new pair of shoes a new set of rings to show me, talking with eagerness and animation of anything that was new and bright, and never, never referring to family, tradition, custom, superstition, all that I dredged now. I was certain she hated such talk as much as I did, even if she had no reason to fear them. Such things simply did not step over the bright enamelled horizon of her painted world, for such things bore shadows, and shadows were alien to her at once, in a similar world, if a richer and more refined one, they had been alien to me, who now constantly looked behind to see where the purple ghost of the albino followed on silk-swathed, oil softened feat. (61)

Anita Desai's use of contrasting outlooks of her characters on matters of horoscope, fatalism, love, life and reality shows her authorial address to the reader. If Maya believed in prophecy as the basic structure which governs lives, Gautama is "a disbeliever." Indeed he fastidiously challenges Harbans Singh, his friend, on the efficacy of prophecy.

> No educated adult can seriously be expected to believe that the patterns of the movements of the astral bodies, solids, after all, of earth and ice and rock—or the lines formed in the palms of your hands, and in those of monkeys and gorillas, as well, have the remotest influence upon our deeds and actions in our everyday lives—or those of the apes. (79)

The technique of abstract notions like fate is characterized with concrete situation. Raisahab is a born fatalist and has learnt that there is no way to escape it. Maya becomes a fatalist after Toto's death; Leila relinquishes all action of life as mere fatalism. Gautama is a postmodern thinker, an "optimist" in reconciling reality and idealism. Talking on these basic things to Maya, he says:

> Like most young people, you cannot understand that reality and idealism is one and the same thing. Life is not a matter of distinguishing the two, but of reconciling them. (21)

Gautama's anticlimax of love is described as,

> That one day we would spurn, love—the splendid ideal of the young—ultimately becomes, you will find for the man a matter or dealing with the bills that come in, and, for the woman, of worrying about them. (21)

In the same vein, it is interesting to watch Gautama expound on the superfluity of death as a search for replacement.

> As for death—Toto's dying, you find, you will become a matter of missing the games you played with him, finding empty time heavy on your hand and, ultimately, a search for replacement. It is rather shocking to reduce one's ideals to mundane superfluities, and equally shocking to realize that these superfluities are the ideals themselves. (21)

The conflict of the Western and Asian philosophy pointed by Raisahab provides undertones to the character of Maya. Raisahab explains in simple terms to Maya:

> The source of disintegration is the human being's vanity in her power to act. . . . The world is born of the western theory of life, not an Asian one. We have been taught for generations to believe that the merit of accepting one's limitation and acting within them is greater than that of destroying them and trying to act beyond them. (54-55)

Symbolism in Anita Desai's novels enhances the psychic tension of the characters. The writer studies her characters like a psychiatrist and depicts their moods through symbols. In *Cry, the Peacock*, Maya seeks a cultural change through reflection and interior monologue mainly through symbols. The title *Cry, the Peacock* has evoked several meanings to the Indian and western critics.

Peacock is the metaphor of love and death mystifying a demonic feminine desire. Maya's self-conscious desire stresses the irony of the tradition. The peacock's wild dance constitutes an over-excited sensibility of Maya through animal imagery. Anita Desai excels in her literary description and narratorial interpretation when Maya's desire reaches a fever pitch and exhibits a kind of violence on the tender jasmine buds.

> That the gardener had plucked from the down fresh ledges that morning for me to thread into garlands for my hair and wrests, and which, for some reason, I had forgotten. There they lay, almost palpitating with living breath, open, white, virginal. I plunged my face into them and kissed them with a wild longing to pierce through that unimpeachable immaculate chastity of whiteness, to the very soul of their maddening fragrance. What dreams they conjured in swirl of scent, what passions, what scenes of love and farewell. . . . I tore myself away from them, having bruised them with my kisses, and trembling, flung them . . . which was now terrorized by the vast, purple shadows of a dreadful night. (106-7)

Indeed such an overt narration of the grotesque probing the inner psyche reflects a postmodern reality resulting out of the contemporary values. The moonlit night intensifies and distills the real Maya. The dramatic effect of the scene blinds Maya and she pushes Gautama off the roof:

> At the parapet edge, I paused, made him pause, and his words were lost to me as I saw the moon's vast, pure surface, touched only faintly with petals of shadow . . . casting its reflection. (208)

And Gautama makes a fatal mistake:

> His last, decisive one. In telling, gesturing he moved in front of me, thus coming between me and the worshipped moon, his figure an ugly, crooked grey shadow that transgressed its sorrowing chastity, 'Gautama!' I screamed in fury, and thrust out my arms towards, him, out of him, into him and past him, saw him fell then, pass through an immensity of air down to the very bottom. (208)

Maya's masked intention to kill Gautama is heightened in the poetic language of her action. Every word, image, morbid sensation reveals Maya's neurotic mind and fear of death predicted by the astrologer.

> Wild horse, white horse, galloping up paths of stone, flying away into the distance, the wild hills. The heights, the dizzying, heights of my mountains, towering, tapering edged with cliff-edges, founded on rock. Fall, fall, gloriously fall to the bed of the raining rivers, foaming seas. Horrid arms, legs, tentacles thrashing, blood flowing eyes glazing. Storm . . . storm at sea, at land! Fury whip lash fly furiously. Dangers! (180)

The names of the characters in *Cry, the Peacock* are symbolic. Gautama foregrounds the notion of Gautama Buddha as a spiritually enlightened person with a philosophic resignation to life. Maya is illusion and is caught in the illusion of reality appropriating life in the common world. Arjuna, Maya's brother, is symbolically the voice of conscience. Also the novel is full of symbols portraying the different moods and emotions of fear, longing, darkness between the stars, forlorn evenings, the "drum beats" evoking the image of Lord Shiva's dance of death; lavish burial of death of a rich man as a glorious memory to posterity; Leila as a reminder of "poppies" to Maya; the barren "orchids," "snakes" revealing her erotic desires; "the monkeys" and the caged life; the "dust-storms," "clouds" and "rain," the "horror of copulation"—all describe and address Maya's state of mind. Anita Desai makes the complexities of problematic women transparent and drags them into a fictive narrative.

In *Voices in the City* the characters and the city of Calcutta become the necessary inescapable social reality, where the characters are looking for the possibility of isolation and escape from the totality which seminally contributes to the discourse of postmodernism. The pressures of unrelenting city:

> Thus although one may be tempted to consider Nirode as the hero of the novel, the city of Calcutta is indeed the invisible protagonist of the novel. Calcutta, conceived as a force of creation, preservation and destruction is ultimately identified as a symbol for the Goddess Kali.[5]

Calcutta is critiqued by Anita as a monster city implying the effect of colonization. Amla feels repulsion to the monster city.

> That this monster city that lived no normal healthy, red blooded life but one that was subterranean, under lit, stealthy and odorous of mortality, had captured and enchanted—or disenchanted with her sister and brother. (150)

The symbolic word monster reflects all the antagonistic feelings of the characters involved. Calcutta is merged as ugly, filled with putrefaction, squalor and adversity.

> Beating his way out of the swarming apathy of Howrah, Nirode strode down the bridge, dodging the traffic that made the bridge roar and rattle beneath his feet like a tunnel of bones and steel. Trains crashed murderously past him handcarts rolled recklessly, maniacally by. (7)

Callous, dull, weary, vacant awfully battered and shattered, Calcutta is choked with dirt and darkness, poverty and disease to give an impression of alienation. Calcutta in the pages of Monisha's diary is described as the "city without conscience." The historical narration of Calcutta and its diminishing values present a moving picture of desolation and decay. While the voices recount the misery of Calcutta, Anita Desai attempts to convey the hollow social structures beyond the voices through fictional narrative. The suffocating and stifling environs of Calcutta fill one with exhaustion and despair. It demolishes love, thrill and excitement and all familial relationships.

Where Shall We Go This Summer? portrays the symbolic battle between nature and civilization, Sita, the protagonist, finds the big city of Bombay intolerably violent and her heart pines to go back to Manori, the island-home of her father. She is shocked to see the miserable condition of the house as lifeless and dead. What remains of the house is only "coldness," "white ashes" and "waste," "shrouded in death": The flourish of words is picturesque as Keatsian imagery:

> the cold remains of the bonfire her father had lit here to blaze. Ashes, white and waste. Dust lay as casually as sand on a beach; spider webs spanned the corners of the unfurnished rooms like skeletal palm leaves. (28)

Sita is like a Shakuntala who wishes to live in the lap of nature giving all heart and tenderness against her husband and children who symbolize mind and reason. She can't repudiate her family or dissolute her love for Manori. Anita Desai skillfully denaturalizes this experience through a series of incidents that is emphasized through the abundant use of adjectives and verbs. Sita's refrain her from giving birth to her child in Bombay.

> In many ways her experience of life had been bleak and drab, grey in many ways, harrowing and depressing and she could not bear the thought of bringing the child into a world as dreadful as this.[6]

Manori islands become a symbol of murky past. Against this setting the unusual juxtapositions of the cow and its pollution brighten Desai's language to be more than uniquely Indian: Moses is described as neighing like the "goats," and his eyes like "porpoises." Sita's desire to be free is manifested in her fascination with the foreigner she meets on the roadside. The novel permeates with arresting metaphors. Sita can slip into the fisherman's net with great ease to give a sense of immediacy and dramatic effect to the scene described. Her father's charisma in life is symbolic of the tired Indian woman and her traditional role. It is similar to the politicians who play their part as spell casters, frauds and then delineate.

The use of images, especially of animal images and comparisons to the human characters are extremely suggestive of the true nature of characters. Some of the images are: Nirode working in a "fox or weasel like" fashion; crowded coffee-houses described as "glued," "like flies"; Nirode's wallowing of literature to his "pig-heart's content," Jit's words are issued as a "serpent's forked tongue"; Sunny is described as a "trained baboon"; David and Dharma as "marsh birds"; Nirode as "a broken bird"; "an unshelled snail," etc. There are powerful images related to crabs, cobras, rats and bats. Dharma defines Amla's instincts as "butterfly" instincts and hence advises her when she ought to "fly," "rest," "go" and "return." Such images abound the novel in a cyclical narration.

In *Fire on the Mountain,* Raka is symbolically an intruder, an outsider, "a mosquito flown up from the plains to tease and worry." (40) The girl has already seen the harsh realities of life, the city of Chandigarh, dull and metallic like a "snake's eye watching" (49) and her abusive father beat her mother which has an impact on the vulnerable, innocent girl. Her unspeakable torture is conveyed through the scars and scratches on her body:

> She would return with her brown legs, scratched, her knees bruised, sucking a finger stung by nettles, her hair brown under a layer of dust, her eyes very still and thoughtful as though she had visited strange lands and seen fantastic improbable things that lingered in the mind. (46)

Ramlal, the cook is a man with a deep desire to save the girl; he engages her with adventurous stones and approaching sandstorms. Nanda Kaul and Raka talk about escaping each other. The story line is thin. Nanda Kaul tells Raka fairytales and stories of her father, lies in order to captivate Raka into her love. Though she hates to take responsibility, deep in her heart Nanda Kaul yearns for love of her people. Jasbir Jain describes the use of fantasy:

> Self-revelation is not the main thrust of fantasy on *Fire on the Mountain* which uses it in an entirely different way. It is not bordering on hallucination. Two kinds of fantasy would exist side by side, one which is consciously and deliberately woven by Nanda Kaul to interest her great grandfather Raka, the other which is shared by Raka and Ramlal and is based on his belief in the supernatural. . . . Raka's private world of fantasy is somewhere between the two—it is neither wholly and naturally accepted fact as the Churails are for Ramlal, nor is it a lie woven for self-preservation. In *Fire on the Mountain*, fantasy also exists purely at the level of imagery as a part of the self-analysis which some of the characters carry on.[7]

Anita Desai uses natural imagery to define the character of Nanda Kaul—with her children—all alien to her nature, and her husband—who betrayed her all her life, Nanda Kaul wishes to be a tree.

> That she could merge with the pine trees and be mistaken for one. To be a tree, no more and no less, was all she was prepared to undertake. (1)

The girl's abnormal behaviour begins with the fear of the forest fires. Raka is appalled like Nanda Kaul.

The emotionally disturbed self and her desire to escape to a harmonious world is projected in G.M. Hopkins' lines to be away into a world "where no storms come" and "where the green earth smells." It is Nanda Kaul's desire and indeed is Anita Desai's basic and objective correlative for such a life:

> I have desired to go whose springs not fail,
> To fields where flies no sharp and sided hail
> And a few lilies blow
> And I have asked to be

> Where no storms come,
> where the green swell is in the heaven's dumb
> And out of the swing of the sea. (58)

Nirode, Monisha and Mrs. Chadha live in their prison-house of languished thoughts. Nirode cannot accept his mother's love crusade with the retired Major, abandoning the unsightly apparition of his father.

> something distracted her, footsteps, a voice and she turned to greet, with a ravishing smile, her neighbour, that retired Major, or Brigadier who, with his bestial jaws and small eyes and hairy hands repelled Nirode, made him shrink away watching the large bumbling creative grope at the garden gate, walk past the clump of bamboo dehhas, then the pear tree, the row of azaleas, to where his mother sat on the verandah, smiling a slow, sensual smile. Hideous to see in his mother, hideous to see in the heroine who had led his crusade. (27-28)

Nirode's mother's escape from the burden of family responsibilities is to escape from the crowd, privacy and violence in the city of Calcutta. She is incapable of regenerating of love to her family. It is a larger crisis of a wounded old civilization that makes her life inadequate. Prof. Bose tells Nirode a fable from *Panchatantra*, of four scholarly Brahmins who are anxious to test their knowledge over a dead lion. Three out of the four decide to put life into the dead lion in order to test their scholarship; while the fourth, the only sensible person warns his friends against the dangerous act. And they refuse. The fourth scholar saves his own life by climbing a tree top while the rest are devoured by the lion. The fable, apart from lending an Indian colour semantically interprets Prof. Bose's warning to Nirode on the publication of the magazine *Voices*. Prof. Bose represents the voice of experience who wants to save Nirode from despair and fragmentation. This use of fable from the ancient classic like *Panchatantra*, though not by the author herself, but by one of the characters—make the narration technique postmodern. The use of multiple narratives here adds to the complex style and reiterates the point of view of the author once again.

The strolling musicians singing with oblique allusions to shame Monisha is in the nature of a mimetic representation where a truth is told in a "song to tantalize a woman's flaw. Conversely, the singer constructs a song to entertain the crowds with the facts hinted. Anita Desai weaves this strong sense of the theatrical and circus watching instinct present in the Indian families through her narratives. Postmodernists condemned the parading of woman's flaws—a convention which begets from the politics of misrepresentation.

Anita Desai uses Indian words as inevitable and spontaneous utterances in the routine of these characters. The words in this category are Indian foods like papadums, halwa, char-chari, pooja, etc. Filtering through the English usage, Indian warmth too is exuberated through words like hai, hai, yar, paji Arebaba, Namak Haram etc. Similarly, we get a taste of cockney dialect. Drinka Pinta milka day (*Bye-Bye* 112)

This 'chutnification' of English is a postmodernist device used by many contemporary Indian English novelists. It was a deliberately adapted device by the Indian English writer who resists the imperial canonical use of language. Adit's oppressive attitude towards Sarah warns of the dreadful dimension of a non-Englander towards a native. It is revealed in Adit's attitude towards Sarah:

> She's used to being woken up. These English wives are quite manageable really, you know. Not as fierce as they look—very quiet and hardworking as long as you treat them right and roar at them regularly once or twice a week. (29)

Sarah is equally cold to her inconsiderate husband. Anita Desai uses images to define her characters from real life. Sarah evokes the image of a tortoise out of water.

> Striding down Laurel Lane, her satchel swinging from one shoulder and her long hair caught in tortoise shell band on the nape of her neck, she had the hurried rush and tough brightness of one suspicious, one on the defensive. (30)

Sarah's marital conflict cannot be resolved in London or in India. Exiled and changing roles, her dream is only a "dream." The sound of the birds echoes the sense of this melancholia. Adit thinks himself as a "thrush bird" which,

> flew out of its nest in the pear tree which Dev had unintentionally disturbed and, in a panicked windmill of brown feathers. (157)

There is a periodic shift of Dev's fear of English to settling down in London. And so he,

> walks the streets and parks of the city, grateful for its daffodil patches of sunshine, loathing its sooty, sodden dampness. Eats to flee apples in Pettiwal Lane and fishes limp sausages out of pods of fat in Lyons Corner House. Lies in the grass under the green canopies of Kew Gardens, and narrowly escapes being run over and crushed to death twenty times over Piccadilly Circus. Stands in the dark, wistfully gazing at the peacock-blue and rose-red paper flowers in a Mexican boutique, then is enthralled by the massive, blank bulk of Battersea power station. . . . It is a strange summer, in which he is the bewildered alien, the charmed observer, the outraged outsider and thrilled sightseer all at once and in succession. (95-96)

Adit's fictive love of London is described:

> I like the Covent Garden Opera House. I like the girls here. I like their nylon stockings and the way their noses tilt upwards. . . . I like steamed pudding with treacle. I like—I like thatched cottages and British history—economic freedom! Social freedom. . . . I like strawberries in summer. I like a weekend at the seaside. I even like the BBC! (20-21)

But later, the indifferent Londoners repel him to yearn for his motherland. The fascination for London is symbolic when Dev occupying Adit's flat sings in a palpably alliterative style.

> Make my bed and light the light,
> I'll assume late tonight
> Blackbird, bye bye. (230)

Equally persistent in beat are Adit's lines while departing from London for India:

> Pack up all my cares and woe,
> Here I go, singing low,
> Bye, Bye, Blackbird
> Where somebody cares for me, sugar is sweet and so is she,
> Bye, bye Blackbird. (190)

Shiv. K. Kumar, commenting on Anita Desai's style says: "The sentences meander on, as usual, in response to some inscrutable rhythm, tapering off into mere nothingness."[8]

The novel *Where Shall We Go This Summer?* reveals the ironical shades of Sita's mind who like her namesake suffers in exile when away from her husband and children because of the intense memories or materially distances herself when living with her family. The house, the sea, the islanders, the children, the disturbances of external nature, the monsoon, the birds, the jelly fish, attachments and detachments indicate the world full of violence and destruction. Sita accepts the reality of life and joins her husband, with the ghost of the past left behind. The contrast of her life in the island and Bombay confuse her. The monologue of her soul reflects:

> Which half of her life was real and which unreal. Which of her selves was true, which false? (153)

Like the Indian social tradition, as in all narratives, the novel ends on the note that life is not an escape from reality but acceptance of reality. Sita's husband Raman believes that life must be continued in "all its business." He is a conformist, the ideal father who is loved and respected by his children. He ponders:

> To certain people there comes a day when they must say the great Yes or great No. He who has the Yes ready within him reveals himself at once, and saying it crosses over to the path of honour and his own conviction. (139)

The transformation of Sita is like poetic justice to her husband. In short Desai's women characters are highly effective in their words and temperament. Sita's recollection of the lines of D.H. Lawrence conveys a subtle meaning. Sita has erred and transgressed her role as a mother. She is in need of love; she cannot suffer the alienation of her husband or miss the love of her children. The lines have an epiphanic effect:

> The wild young heifer, glancing distraught,
> With a strange, new knocking of life at her side
> Runs seeking a loneliness.
> The little grain draws the earth to hide,
> Nay, even the slumberous egg, as it labours under the shell.
> Patiently to divide and subdivide.
> Asks to be hidden, and wishes nothing to tell. (150)

As a postmodern writer Anita Desai is making a plea to men that though women have errors they should accept them that "one cannot survive in this world without compromises." It is a sort of warning in a postmodern situation where divorces are common, and where spouses spoil their lives for lack of understanding for each other.

Eliot's subtitle *Fire on the Mountain* in *The Wasteland* uses rhetorical style that evokes external nature and psychic traits of her characters. It is just, words—words in tangled sentence—structures, forcing the reader into a sort of insensateness.[9]

Nanda Kaul's love of Carignano, its "barrenness," and "emptiness" and her desire to live a life without "attachments." Every tree, insect, bird, hills in and around Kasauli exaggerate this attitude of Nanda Kaul. Her life is symbolically portrayed through a creeper hanging on the wooden railing:

> The yellow rose creeper had blossomed so youthfully last month but was now reduced to an exhausted mars of grey creeks and groans against.[10]

She has discharged her family duties and desires to be free like the eagle,

> far below her, a thousand feet below, its wings outspread, gliding on currents of air without once moving its greet muscular wings which remained in repose, in control. (19)

She does not like the babble of Ila Das to meet her since she has been thrust by her daughter Asha to keep Raka, her great grand-daughter. Nanda Kaul has been forced by her selfish and loveless children into loneliness and now she can't accept Raka's prospective arrival into her "pared, reduced and radiantly single life." (31)

Anita Desai's language is the language of the inner world of her characters. The use of poetic lines is Anita Desai's technique of illuminating the meaning of life. In poetry there is life, a life without poetry is dead.

Anita Desai's technique is to provide the nature of reality and its complexity through the art of writing. Art is connected with the reality of life, human nature and vision of life are riddled with illusion and society. Man's anxiety to immortalize Art through technology is a farce.

Deven's love for Nur's poetry in *In Custody* stands for unexpressed love for his father. The art of writing according to Anita Desai is mentioned at the outset of the discussion on technique,

> A writer does not create a novel by observing a set of theories—he follows flashes of individual vision. (16)

Mirpore is like an "impressionist painting," it "lacked history, the town had probably existed for centuries in its most basic, most elementary form." (19) For all his worthwhile work Deven's dream is broken. Deven is a dreamer. He gets a chance to undertake the task of featuring an interview with the living and greatest poet, Nur. His entire mission is beset with appearance and reality. If Deven thinks that Urdu poet should be like a God and his words full of poetry, "beauty" and "illumination," he is shocked to be encountered by:

> Who is it that *disturbs* the sleep of the aged at this hour of the afternoon that is given to rest? It can only be a great fool. Fool, are you a fool. (13)

Deven as a dreamer cannot confront the reality of life. He naturally embitters his wife Sarla who believes that marriage is connected with "fax," "phone," "refrigerator" and a "car." She is angry and embittered at her husband. She can be a great sulker when she retires to her kitchen,

> It was only when she had disappeared into this narrow, cluttered fastness of hers and could be heard freely rattling and clattering in there that it occurred to Deven. (127)

If his marriage is miserable, Nur's married life is hollow and loveless.

If to Imtiaz Begum 'art' is a means to earn money and livelihood, to Nur and Deven it needs total and selfless dedication. Deven fails to capture Nur's poetry because of professional incompetence and lack of technical skill. Nur is trapped in the bitter responsibilities and restrictions of his wives. Ironically Nur and Deven are trapped in the clamouring chaotic family drama.

If Mr. Abid Siddiqui's help to arrange funds from the college authorities rouses Deven's hopes to record the interview, he is terribly disappointed over Chiku's failure to record Nur's voice on time. The novel weathers through celebration and agony. Deven dreams "that in capturing Nur's poetry all his socio-economic problems would be solved. Deven realizes that poetry, man's dream world, is absolutely ideal and if it were made real,

> then the bubble would be breached and burst, and it would no longer be perfect. And if it were not perfect, and constant, then it would all have been for nothing, it would be nothing. (166)

Though the interview fails Deven's relationship with Nur, it ironically binds him to an unforeseen responsibility to be the custodian of Nur's poetry and his clamouring family. Deven thinks that perhaps the poet's death would end the clamour-ridden burden. But it indomitably binds him to Nur's very soul and spirit. He accepts Nur's poetry because he cannot abandon under pressure. The novel ends with an optimistic note: "Soon the sun would be up blazing." (204) This dispels the fears and regenerates a possible change from the present condition. His life is filled with benign happiness. Deven runs to accept this "distinction."

> He had accepted the gift of Nur's poetry and that meant he was custodian of Nur's very soul and spirit. It was a great distinction. (178)

Clear Light of Day is a passage of time with the characters moving from present to the past. It leads to the surfacing of the unconscious, the uncovering of many forgotten episodes or the forgotten nuances of the incidents in the lives of Bim and Tara and the causes for their own behaviour. Slowly as the past is reviewed, a metamorphosis of attitude occurs. Repetition, reenactment and recollection, thus become a technique of narration in Desai's hands. Bim recalls the historical past of the summer of 1947 where she reflects:

> There are these long still stretches, nothing happens and then suddenly there is a crash . . . and then life subsides again into the back waters till the next push, the next flood. (42)

The memory lives in *Cry, the Peacock* or the multiple narrations in *Voices in the City*; island interlude in *Where Shall We Go This Summer?*; the four parts of *Clear Light of Day* are the narrative strategies. Mrs. Chadha's playing the role of high-priestess at a ritual sacrifice; Sita packing the suitcases as if the stage had been cleared for the players to go home; Sarah feeling as an imposter in the role of the English Secretary and equally as the Indian wife as in the real world are the role plays of the protagonists.

Though Sita and Sarah play roles, Bim in *Clear Light of Day* resents the idea of fitting into roles or roles being thrust on people. If she feels ridiculous at the suggestion that Raja should step into her father's shoes and take up family responsibility, and is unhappy about the role thrust on Aunt Mira. She could not grasp the disturbed atmosphere of their lives. She overcomes the confused condition of her mind. It begins with the study of the life of Aurangzeb, which indeed makes her think about her life again. She is highly impressed by the sentences:

> Many were around me when I was born. But now I am going alone 'and' . . . strange that I came with nothing into the world, and now go away with this stupendous caravan of sin. (165)

She consciously tries to stay out of the role of a sacrificing elder sister. In Anita Desai's novels, roles become facades clouding the characters from reality to bind them into a certain behavioural pattern. Often social norms thrust roles on people to outgrow their social premise. But if the required courage and determination is not exhibited, they end in alienation and self-dissociation. Role transformation at times may be the result of some emotional experience as well, when the character becomes indifferent to social claims, like Nirode's mother, who is bereaved with the death of Monisha. Her life had been vibrant, colourful and unfulfilled with an apparition-like husband and loveless children. Monisha's death supplies the tragic dimension from which she has no chance of expression.

It is this philosophic dimension and a deepening mystery that she appears a magnificent portrait in a great tragedy. Indeed Nirode, the "snail without shell," is engulfed with compassion for his mother whom he hated. Bim's role in life had changed due to external circumstances and shows little rebellion or opposition to the growth of her character. Bim grows into an ennobling character with the enlightenment from inside without any tragic dimension. Anita Desai uses the technique of rebellion and non conformity. The use of images and metaphors are unconventional and often subversive of the established sense of reality. Anita Desai uses the technical devices that give apt expression to the sense they are necessary for the development of character. If rebellion is an indication of will power and ego, it becomes an act of division rather than of polarity, an obsession rather than confrontation. Monisha's rebellion is one sided. She silently accepts defeat, accepts solitude as a true gift which no communication or art or faith or delusion can offer, and finally it is acceptance which destroys her.

Anita Desai uses the technique of movement of mind between childhood and adulthood to show a certain flexibility of attitude. It is this fluidity of movement that helps the growth of Bim.

Children also play an important role in the development of the meaning in the novels of Anita Desai. Das children in *Clear Light of Day* are different from the Rays. Though childhood is not a condition they'd like to return to, there is every need and desire to think about it. Childhood, according to Anita Desai is important in the manner in which it influences adult responses, but also because children comprehend things better than adults. Bim recollects her childhood days, the games played, the dreams dreamt, and the hours spent staring at the stars with such clarity, without her senses being distorted by age. Indeed the presence or absence of children shows the difference to the quality of thought, to hope or dismalness of life.

Positively, it is the children who dispel the ghosts by their curiosity to visit haunted places. Raka's wild wanderings force Nanda Kaul to review her past. It is through the memory of children that Bim and Tara take stock of their lives. Sita's return to Bombay, in other words to her sanity is brought about by Menaka. Contrasted to them are Sarla and Jaya (*Clear Light of Day*), the childless and abandoned women who ironically run a school for children whom they detest in the same grooves.

In Anita Desai's novels, childhood attitudes and experiences constitute the "core" character which surfaces the world of the unconscious. The moment the unconscious comes into play, the idea of a consistent, integrated character becomes valid. Also as the experiences occur or are analyzed, different aspects of the same person are revealed, some which are incognizant and some which are discovered.

To Anita Desai, every fresh occurrence brings about a change of perspective and formation of the character which is cumulative process of revision and retraction. The different dimensions of the characters projected are the different selves of the character revealing a plurality and secrecy in relation to time, like the way Monisha views the past as lingering like a "long twilight" into the present. It is a past which cloys which has to be preserved with its lingering essence.

To the questions what time, why history, to what purpose, Anita Desai relates that both time and history are important for the personal and collective experience of an individual. It is time that establishes the connection between character and narration, between individual and event, in Anita Desai's novels. In the family drama of life, the past and present of the character are never really separate but are fused into one. The role of freedom and lack of educational opportunities too have a technical significance.

In *Clear Light of Day* lack of freedom and lack of opportunities, rights of inheritance are ubiquitous like the Bengali women behind barred windows in *Voices in the City*. *Clear Light of Day* is a landmark in Anita Desai's career. It marks a "breaking point" in her use of language where she incorporates the rhythm and tone of Indian speech. The effect has been described by Gabriella Annan in the *Times Literary Supplement* as "Four Dimensional."

Anita Desai makes fun of the bureaucrats by portraying first Jiban (*Voices in the City*) and then Bakul (*Clear Light of Day*) with narrow and limited imagination, of disinterested academicians and teachers in men like Deven (*In Custody*). Though religion invades language, literature, art and education, religion has a marginal role in Anita Desai's novel because of its failure for sustenance and succour. English is the language of communication and correspondence in the Ray family and with Mrs. Chadha. Murad's attempts to run an Urdu magazine and publish Nur's poetry become a heroic theme seeking political patronage.

The intensities of the English language fascinate the writer not only as communication but as imagery and as a means of description of events and happenings. Adjectives, phrases, images abound in Anita Desai's novels to weave a pattern of meaning—horny thumbs, unthinking bees, shriveling again, like mother lead in a groove cut into earth etc. (5-6)

In *Voices in the City*, Anita Desai's language follows a similarly rich style but gradually the language becomes more controlled and much more finely honed down. In *In Custody*, language is loaded with irony.

Monisha's suicide, Mira Masi's drunken experiences, Maya's response to Arjuna are full of lingering memories. In Anita Desai's novels, the Freudian undercurrents and fragmentary vignettes illustrate the multi-faceted nature of reality. What remains is the unknown quantity of reality and the mysterious, stubborn elusive self. Sita's desire to go to Manori islands is in the likeness of the opening chapters of Daphine Du Mauner's *Frenchman's Greek* as an impulsive escape from the routine of womanhood and shows Anita Desai's literary device relating the Indian and Western culture. But the binding values of woman as a wife and mother dominate the impulsive act to escape from the routine of womanhood. Sita in this novel and the other lady characters display their strong affinity to the culture they were born in and brought up. In Anita Desai's novels, it is ultimately the subservient attitude of women which recurs and leaves little hope that the ladies would ever become what they long for. Despite being born in the country where a woman like Indira Gandhi was born, these women remain the same throughout. It may take some more time for them to play the role that Indira Gandhi advocates for women.

> Woman must be a bridge and a synthesizer. She shouldn't allow herself to be swept off her feet by superficial trends nor yet be chained to the familiar. She must ensure the continuity which strengthens roots and simultaneously engineer change and growth to keep society dynamic, abreast of knowledge, sensitive to fast moving events. The solution lies neither in fighting for equal posi-

tion nor denying it, neither in retreat into the home nor escape from it.[11]

The processes of creation and destruction, the constant flow of past and present, the violence which disintegrates to create a new pattern, repetition, re-enactment and recollection and everything that recovers the central identity of the self are methods of narration in Anita Desai's novels. The fictional techniques become not only concrete methods aimed at visible results towards acceptance of life but also are imaginative explorations constantly recreating and redefining reality, contributing to the moment of social realism.

NOTES

1. Anita Desai, "Replies to the Questionnaire," *Kakatiya Journal of English Studies*, Vol. III, No. 1, pp. 1-2.
2. Graham A. Allan, *A Sociology of Friendship and Kinship* (London: George James, Allen and Unwin, 1979), p. 92. Rpt. in Usha Pathania, *Human Bonds and Bondages: The Fiction of Anita Desai and Kamala Markandaya* (place?? Kamakshi, 1992), p. 1.
3. Henry James, *The Art of the Novel: Critical Prefaces*, with an Introduction by Richard P. Blackmur (New York: Scribner, 1962), p. 120.
4. R.S. Sharma, *Anita Desai* (New Delhi: Arnold Heinemann, 1981), 167.
5. A.V. Krishna Rao, "*Voices in the City*, A Study," *Perspectives on Anita Desai*, ed. Ramesh K. Srivastava (Ghaziabad: Vimal, 1984), p. 175.
6. Jasbir Jain, "Work of Some Length": An Interview with Anita Desai, *Stairs to the Attic: The Novels of Anita Desai* (Jaipur: Printwell, 1987), p. 11.
7. Jasbir Jain, "The Use of Fantasy in Anita Desai's Novels," *Explorations in Modern Indo-English Fiction*, ed. R.K. Dhawan (New Delhi: Bahri, 1982), pp. 227-37.
8. Shiv K. Kumar, "The Fiction of Anita Desai: Another View," *The Humanities Review*, III, 2 (January-December 1981), pp. 43-46.
9 Shiv. K. Kumar, p. 194.

10. Anita Desai, *Fire on the Mountain* (New Delhi: Allied, 1985), p. 17.
11. Amarnath Prasad, "A Brief History of Indian Women Novelists in English," *Indian Women Novelists in English* (New Delhi: Atlantic, 2001), p. 1.

Chapter VI

Conclusion

'Postmodern' calls for a change in the attitude and habits which reflect the codified behaviour that is widespread from self to society to nation. It is necessarily a reaction against the canonical notions which clung to the classical norms of the 'Best and the Rest.' Postmodernism questions these norms as they catered to the elite taste of a privileged few and disregarded a vast ocean of humanity. Postmodernism matters today because it offers scope for all. It upholds the egalitarian view that all are born with immense potential—despite caste, creed, race or gender—and each one can blossom into a genius if given chance. Therefore, meta-narratives are deconstructed, conventions are dismantled, culture is remapped and relocated. It welcomes within its range everyone who is willing to contribute—nothing comes amiss—anything goes.

Anita Desai would be defined as a postmodern writer because of her compelling exploration of women's psyche and the social realities. Anita Desai wrote about the discontent and the internal hemorrhage inside the body of Indian society. She wrote in order to uplift the essential dignity of women that despite their errors, they incite compassion in the hearts of men. Anita Desai shows that the women who attempt to transgress male prerogatives often spell disaster. In other words the cry of her heroines is "I want to live." Anita Desai depicts the tension in love through all different facets of human psyche and in all kinds of human relationships. As a feminist postmodern writer, she seeks love, understanding and acceptance of reality in life.

To understand Anita Desai is to understand her women characters. It is the female characters who offer emotional intensity. It is to understand the demons that haunt these women, the motivations that shape them, and the doubts that plague them. And as it goes by the postmodernists norms, Anita Desai's novels require a new literary understanding, and willingness to cope with the changing situation.

Anita Desai's characters are existential in the dimension of life and psychoanalytic in the exploration of mind. Her women are intense, complex and riddled with seemingly irreconcilable contradictions whose detours and flashbacks add to the kernel of truth. True to her women characters, Anita Desai draws from inside in her search for the true meaning of life. They are a continuing discourse on postmodernism. The discourse is felt through the voices of her characters: Monisha, Maya, Nanda Kaul, Sita, Bim, Sarah and Lotte. It is the discourse that makes known the real world of women and the justice they seek in the first place. Such a world as this could be created with the postmodern possibilities.

If convention demands that a Maya should not pine or whine for physical fulfillment and should suppress such desires, the postmodernist questions such a premise which works on an individual and deconstruct the convention. In other words, postmodernism allows for a free play of such repressed desires. It attacks the conventional claims about truth, ethics and beauty, which suppress biological urges and desires. According to Anita Desai every individual has an inherent ability to discover the meaning of life. It is the failure of the socio, economic, cultural, politico, intellectual, spiritual and psychological forces that make women suffer more.

Maya lives in an unconventional society where she has no freedom to express her desire. With the disturbing experience of Nur's wives, Deven in *In Custody* recognizes that dismissal of women, i.e., dismissal of the noisy bawling wives of Nur means failure of Nur's poetry. Desai is trying to point out that it is fundamental to Indian society that women are dependent on men. The shabby sullen appearance of Sarla is also a part of the unfortunate woman like Nur's wives. Deven strides forward to carry the burden not with a gesture of pain but with robust optimism. It is a postmodern expression of writer writing about the predicament of an emerging writer. This is a significant juncture in the ongoing debate on postmodernism that gives *In Custody* a dignity and moral stature. Ironically the novel is a postmodern expression of Nur's poetry against the poetry of women. That postmodernist criticism attacks the social structures which operate towards the oppression of women is the success of the postmodernist movement.

Anita Desai, in attempting to assert independence to these unfortunate women, gives voice to women who are trapped in isolation in the confines of husband and family. It is a whole reconstruction and positioning of women on the social structure who have lost their voice in the countless generations of womanhood that postmodern writers are precisely aiming to write about.

Anita Desai feels that woman is a trapped animal and lives in an illusion that she had discovered the trap door without realizing that it is a door to another trap. Unless a woman expresses her need, there can be no freedom for woman. Most of Anita Desai's novels have this kind of climactic endings and demand answers from the readers. Conclusive forms vanish. Anita Desai's words remain.

Anita Desai employs distinct narrative techniques with rhythm and pattern moving from past to present in a linear or circular manner. Metaphorically it is a passage from childhood to adulthood, from subjugation to freedom, from trauma to creativity or from colonization to decolonization. This movement in and out of Time as technical device is used by several contemporary writers of fiction. Salman Rushdie's *Midnight's Children,* Allan Sealy's *The Trotter Nama* and Githa Hariharan's *Thousand Faces of Night* are some prominent examples. And these novelists are also important contributors to the postmodern novel.

It is through the confines of a novel that we see what it means to be an Indian woman today. In western countries, the women's issues are mostly identity, job equality and sexual roles. In India, for the majority, it is a question of stark survival. The few who have escaped the vicious existential circle through education and better opportunities also find themselves in constant tussle with the inevitable. While survival is important, the aim is to be a whole human being, regardless of difference in sex, colour, religion, caste or country. It is therefore, timely to redress the imbalances and take a close look at women created out of fact by fiction while the bulk of Indian Writing in English is in the novel form, at least the Indian males and female might profitably examine their images within the created compass of a novel, albeit in a male dominated society, by writers, both male and female, of fiction. This is one realm where one could explore the permanent values and not get bogged down by the arguments about sex.

The fictive world would reveal the Indian woman's nature on grounds not only biological, psychological, economic, sociological or political but essentially literary, which may overtake all these modes. An Indian woman is defined by a set of relationships and modes of conduct within a created society. The question of woman's superiority or inferiority to man is irrelevant. What is relevant is the modern Indian woman's effort to grapple with the particular, the immediate. The very real problems of men and women are of the rural women whose labour is unjustly rewarded and who hold little interest for writers. No Indian English writer has dealt with these conditions so far.

If the Indian woman picks up enough courage to raise her head and ask a few awkward but pertinent questions, the responses would shift towards new development strategies in the Indian society. The need of the hour is to portray the Indian woman as they are—shorn of all poetry and romance and fettered by domestic injustice and tyrannical custom. In actual literary practice, most of the women protagonists persistently reenact the suffering and sacrificing role of Sita or Savitri. A classification of the different categories of men and women would bring about a realistic fiction of the postmodern scene.

With the influence of traditional literature in the portrayal of women, the postmodern focuses women who have emerged victorious; women who are struggling to swim through and the women who are rejected, betrayed and defeated. Anita Desai's image of woman has been viewed as being essentially weak creatures constantly requiring the protection of man as their lord and master. Anita Desai makes her female protagonist aware of the factors that condition her life, and these factors are considered as the cause of women's suffering as in India as anywhere else. Thus, Anita Desai's art transcends the immediate context and reaches out to the wider world where women suffer and endeavour to steer out of that suffering. This makes Anita Desai essentially a postmodernist novelist.

Maya cannot cope with her fixity and becomes an irredeemable individual. Monisha is a "stuffed rag doll" who chooses to die than submit to her mean existence. Nirode spurns everything of the upper middle-class existence, dress and food. Sita struggles to reconnect to society. Ila Das, Nanda and Raka wish to forget their painful lives. Jiban is narrow and limited in his understanding of his wife Monisha. Deven lacks professional skill and worldly logic. Gautama is a detached being living in society; Rai Sahab accepts his lot in society. Bim is an urban, independent self-assured individual. She emerges triumphant of all the heroines of Anita Desai, who refuses to be weak-willed, dependent, shy and not become an object for others' use and pleasure.

Anita Desai's characters exhibit the courage to swim against the tide C.P. Cavafy, Anita Desai's favorite Greek poet, reflects her own philosophy and the kind of characters she likes to create

> I am interested in characters who are not average but have retreated or have been driven into some extremity of despair and to turn against or made a stand against the general current. It is easy to flow with the current, it makes no demands, it costs no effort, but those who cannot follow it, whose heart cries out "the great

> No," who fight the current and struggle against it, they know what the demands are and what it costs to meet them.[1]

Cavafy's second part of the poem is well demonstrated by Sita in who has eventually learnt to say 'No' in *Where Shall We Go This Summer?:*

> He who refuses, does not repent should he be asked again, he would say No again. And yet that No—the straight No—crushed him for the rest of his life.[2]

Anita wants men like Raman *(Where Shall We Go This Summer?)* whose philosophy is "Life must be continued, and all its business and children will look up and respect such a man" like the lines of the Cavafy poem.

> To certain people there comes a day when they must say the great Yes or the great No. . . . He who has the Yes ready within him reveals himself at once, and saying it crosses over to the path of honour and his own conviction. (139)

Anita Desai acknowledges her debt to Constantine P. Cavafy's great poem, *The Grand Refusal* which eulogizes courage. Anita Desai uses this poem as a guideline in her characterization and the larger dimension of her own life *in Where Shall We Go This Summer?*

The aim of Anita Desai's novels reflects the characteristic spirit of age which has loosened the relationship of husband and wife and the eventual breakdown of family. Anita Desai's novels have a pattern which matches the rhythms of life. They emerge beyond the barriers of caste, creed and nation to depict the human predicament and the unchanging human destiny. Characters are forced by circumstances or interiorize their feelings as marginalized beings. Anita Desai gives voice to this subaltern victim of multiple marginality to poignantly project their predicament. She explores the nature of human relationship in the changing times. What she states about *Clear Light of Day* should be true of other novels as well:

> My novel is set in Old Delhi and records the tremendous change that a Hindu family goes through since 1947. Basically my preoccupation was with recording the passage of time: I was trying to write a four-dimensional piece on how a family's life moves backwards and forwards in a period of time. My novel is about time as a destroyer, as a preserver and about what the bondage of time does to people. I have tried to tunnel under the mundane surface of domesticity.[3]

The question of self is germane to relations in the family. Self is something to be shared and realized. Childhood sows seeds for this realization. It is a dream and a myth. As Sita feels, future offers a refuge to the identification of self. If inhibitions of the self are unchecked, it creates vulnerability. A psychic residue of the inhibition leads to fear of death and fear of the unknown. This fear leads to the growth of a complex self, as in the case of Maya.

Anita Desai's novels are strewn with characters whose strength is not so enduring. This weakness is more pronounced in women characters. Women are quintessential seekers of self realization and self-fulfillment. When female protagonists negate womanhood and motherhood, they annihilate and immolate themselves like Monisha or regenerate and re-identify themselves as Sita and Bim. According to Anita Desai, life is a quest for identity, a continual process of "sacrifice, adjustment and compromise."

To Anita Desai, finishing one book is like leaving one stage of life or endlessly replacing the same theme. Her *Fasting and Feasting* has been shortlisted for the Booker Prize. It shows her mastery of idiom in handling the complex interpersonal relationships which are becoming highly reactionary in our age. Critics of Anita Desai read *Journey to Ithaca* as a novel more about banishment than about a journey. The journey of the Italian Matteo with his German wife Sophie to meet the Eastern spiritualist Herman Hesse on a hippy train to India examines the reactions that attract and repel India to the westerners. It anticipates a pragmatist pluralism, to think beyond racial problems towards a cultural hybridity.

It is said that postmodernism is over and we live in post-postmodernism times. Thus, Anita Desai, essentially a novelist of our times, writes about the contemporary issues particularly related with Indian women. She has upheld the women's cause throughout her career as a novelist, not as a propagandist, but as a creative writer—an artist who explores the female psyche in order to understand it and relate it to the readers. This is what precisely makes her a postmodern novelist. Modernism never allowed any social issue to creep into its elite jargon. In spite of his defiance against old convention, the modernist artist refused to extend his creative sensibility to any social cause. Issues like social marginality, race and gender, sociology and literature etc. were alien to the modernist art. It was in the postcolonial era that these issues were addressed to and taken up as worthy subject for creative arts. The entire gamus of women's writing, Feminist Literary criticism, Literature of the less privileged (Dalits) in India and elsewhere, African Literature, African-American Literature, Literature of the tribal experience, of the aboriginals, literature of the immigrant experience, issues of multiculturalism, diasporic literature—all these mark a phase in history which is postmodern.

Anita Desai's exploration of the female psyche and the technical devices she uses often tend to be modernist in nature, but modernism, in its defiance of the old conventions, made a way for further digression from the canonical norms. Therefore, when it comes to technicalities, the demarcation line between the two—Modernism and Postmodernism—becomes thinner. The difference lies in the artist's approach to life and literature. The modernist artist was overawed by the changes that had suddenly come upon him at the beginning of twentieth century. He was baffled and uncertain though convincingly aggressive. Postmodernist artist, on the other hand, has learnt to accept those changes as reality. He feels more secure and at ease, and celebrates the surrounding situation. Such technical devices like temporal disorder, pastiche, paranoia etc. can be found in the work of modernist writer as well as in the work of postmodernist ones. Anita Desai's psycho-analysis is one device which can be attributed to both Modernism and Postmodernism. She also makes effective use of such devices as symbolism which has been used by all the great creative artists of the world.

Thus after having considered Postmodernism as an ideology that is akin to our times and having analyzed Anita Desai's novels in the light of this ideology one can conclude that Postmodernism is a contemporary phase of history which emerged out of ideological differences with Modernism that swept the west during the 1920s. Postmodernism encompasses such issues as women's studies, women's literature etc. and encourages women to write about themselves and about the social convention that enslaved them through history. Anita Desai is a product of postmodern conditions—a woman writer of convincing literary merits—she writes basically about the suffering of women, and exposes the factors that caused the suffering. Women are "other" in patriarchy. Anita Desai's treatment of their issues makes her a postmodernist writer.

Anita Desai's art of fiction writing reveals—both thematically and technically—the postmodernist elements that have gone into the making of this art. Anita Desai's contribution to contemporary Indian English Novel, which again is a part of postmodern writing, is unequivocally acknowledged as remarkable.

NOTES

1. Yashodhara Dalmia, "An Interview with Anita Desai," *The Times of India*, April 29, 1979.
2. Anita Desai, *Where Shall We Go This Summer?* New Delhi: Orient Paperbacks.
3. Sunil Sethi, Pieces of the Past, Review of Anita Desai's *Clear Light of Day, India Today*, 5, No. 23, December 1-15, 1980.

Bibliography

Primary Sources

Desai, Anita. *Cry, the Peacock*, London: Peter Owen, 1963. Calcutta: Rupa, 1964. Delhi: Orient Publishers, 1980.

_____. *Voices in the City*, London: Peter Owen, 1965. Delhi: Hind Pocket Books, 1965. Tipatul Panulai, Rumania: Colectia Meridiane, 1968 (in Romanian).

_____. *Bye-Bye, Blackbird,* Delhi: Hind Pocket Books, 1971

_____. *Where Shall We Go This Summer?* Delhi: Vikas, 1975. Delhi: Orient Paperbacks, 1982.

_____. *Fire on the Mountain*, New York: Harper Row, 1977. Delhi: Allied, 1977. London: William Heinemann, 1978. Sweden: Trivi, 1980. Harmondsworth: King Penguin, 1983.

_____. *Clear Light of Day*, London: William Heinemann, 1980. New York: Harper Row, 1980. Harmondsworth: King Penguin, 1983.

_____. *In Custody*, London: William Heinemann, 1984.

_____. *The Village by the Sea*, Delhi: Allied, 1985.

_____. *Baumgartner's Bombay*, London: William Heinemann, 1988.

_____. *Journey to Ithaca,* London: Heinemann, 1995.

Secondary Sources

Acharya, Shanta. "Problems of the Self in the Novels of Anita Desai." *Explorations in Modern Indo-English Fiction*, ed. R.K. Dhawan. New Delhi: Bahri, 1982, pp.236-54.

Adapa, Rama Krisha Rao. "Anita Desai's Modernist Novel," *The Literary Endeavor,* II, 2-3, pp.11-14.

Aithal, S. Krishnamoorthy and Rashmi Aithal. "East-West Encounter in Four Indo-English Novels." *ACLALS Bulletin*, Sixth Series. No. 1 (November 1982), pp.1-16.

Alcock, Peter. "Rope, Serpent, Fire: The Recent Fiction of Anita Desai." *Journal of Indian Writing in English*, Vol. IX, No. 1, Jan. 81, pp.15-34.

Alladi, Uma. "To Accept or Reject: The Woman as Wife." *The Literary Criterion*, Vol. XX, No. 4, 1985, pp. 79-90.

Asnani, Shyam M. "Anita Desai's Fiction: A New Dimension." *Indian Literature*, 24, 2, March-April 1981, pp. 44-54.

Belliappa, Meena. *Anita Desai: A Study of Her Fiction*. Calcutta: Writers Workshop, 1971.

_____. "East-West Encounter: Indian Women Writers of Fiction." *Literary Criterion,* VIII, 3, 1966, 18-27.

Bande, Usha. *The Novels of Anita Desai*. Prestige, New Delhi, 1988.

Banerjee, Surendranath, *Speeches and Writings*; *A Nation in the Making: Reminiscences of Fifty Years in Public Life* (1927).

Bhatt, L. Savita. *Indianness Nayantara and Anita.* Calcutta: Parumita, 2000.

Bullock Oliver, Alan, Stally Brass and Stephen Trombley, ed. *The Fontana Dictionary of Modern Thought.* London: Fontana Press, 1990.

Chadha, Ramesh. *Cross-Cultural Interaction in Indian English Fiction.* New Delhi: National Book Organization, 1988.

Chandrasekharan, K.R. "East and West in the Novels of Kamala Markandaya," *Critical Essays on Indian Writing in English,* ed. M.K. Naik, S.K. Desai and G.S. Amur. Dharwar: Karnataka University, 1968, pp. 62-85.

Choudhury, A.D. *Contemporary British Drama.* Arnold Heinemann.

Cixous, Helene. "The Laugh of Medusa," *New French Feminisms*. New York: Schocken Books, 1981.

Clarkson David. 'Sarah Charlesworth: An Interview' *Parachute* 49:12-15 in Linda Hutcheon's *The Politics of Postmodernism*. Routledge Taylor and Francis Group, London and New York, 41.

Coleman, James C. *Abnormal Psychology and Modern Life* (Bombay: D.B. Tharaporewala, 1981), p. 292.

Cowasjee, Saros. *Studies in Indian and Anglo-Indian Fiction.* New Delhi: Harpercollins, 1993.

Daftry, Nayana. "Review of *Cry, the Peacock.*" *Quest*, Vol. 10, No. 1, Winter 1983, p. 50.

Dalmia, Yashodhara. "An Interview with Anita Desai," *The Times of India*, 29 April 1979.

_____. "Reply to the Questionnaire." *Kakatiya Journal of English Studies*, 3 (1978), 1-6.

Daruwalla, Keki N. "Built on a Non-issue." Review of *In Custody. The Hindustan Times*, 13 Jan. 1985.

Dash, Sandhyarani, *Form and Vision in the Novels of Anita Desai*, Prestige, New Delhi, 1966.

Derrida, Jacques. *Writing and Difference.* Chicago: Chicago University Press, 1978.

_____. *Of Grammatology, trans*. Gayatri Spivak, Baltimore, Md: Johns Hopkins University Press. 1976.

Desai, Anita. "Calcutta Kaleidoscope." *The Illustrated Weekly of India*, 1958.

_____. "Pilgrimage." *The Illustrated Weekly of India*, 1966.

_____. "Women Writers." *Quest*, No. 65. April-June 1970, pp. 39-43.

_____. "The Indian Writers' Problems," *The Literary Criterion*, 12 (Summer 1975), pp. 26-36. Rpt. in *Explorations in Modern Indo-English Fiction*, ed. R.K. Dhawan, New Delhi: Bahri, 1982.

_____. "Reply to the Questionnaire." *Kakatiya Journal of English Studies*, 3 (1978), pp. 1-6.

_____. Interview by Jasbir Jain, *Rajasthan University Studies in English*, 12 (1979), pp. 61-69.

De Souza, Eunice, ed. *Nine Indian Women Poets: An Anthology,* Delhi: Oxford University Press, 1997.

Desani, G.V. *All About H. Hatter* (1948), new edition with an Introduction by Anthony Burgess (1970).

Dhawan, R.K., ed. *The Fiction of Anita Desai*. Bahri, New Delhi, 1989.

Dua, M.R. "Anita Desai." *Femina*, 4 Jan. 1974, p. 25.

Dutt, Charmazel. "Past and Present: A Journey to Confrontation." *Journal of Indian Writing in English*, Vol. IX, No. 1, 1981, pp. 67-73.

DuPlessis, R.B. *Writing beyond the Ending: Narrative Strategies of Twentieth Century Women Writers*. Bloomington: Indiana University Press, 1985. 150:13; 6.

Ford, Boris, ed. *The Pelican Guide to English Literature. The Modern Age*, A Pelican Book, 76.

Foster, Hal, ed. *The Anti-Aesthetic: Essays on Postmodern Culture,* Port Townsend. Wash: Bay Press, 1983.

Foucault, Michael. *The Order of Things: Archaeology of the Human Sciences*, New York: Pantheon, 1970.

_____. *The Archaeology of Knowledge and the Discourse on Language,* trans. A.M. Sheridan Smith, New York: Pantheon, 1972.

_____. *The History of Sexuality: Volume I: An Introduction,* trans. Robert Hurley, New York: Vintage, 1980.

Frow, John. *"What was Postmodernism?"* in Adam and Tiffin (1990)

Gabriel, A. "Anita Desai's *Fire on the Mountain.* A Review," *Times Literary Supplement*, 17 June 1977, p. 721.

Giddens, Anthony. 'Modernism and Postmodernism,' *New German Critique*, 22, 1981, 15-18.

Glendinning, Victoria. "Mood Indigo." Review of *Games at Twilight and Other Stories, Times Literary Supplement*, 1978, p. 973.

Gopal, N.R. *A Critical Study of the Novels of Anita Desai*, Atlantic, New Delhi, 1995, p. 4.

Goyal, Bhagwat S. "The World of Women Novelists," *The Hindustan Times Weekly*, Vol. 4, No. 12, Jan. 69, pp. 64-69.

Habermas, Jurgon. *"Modernity: An Incomplete Project,"* in Foster (1983).

Hariharan, Githa. *The Art of Dying and Other Stories*: New Delhi: Penguin, 1993.

Harvey, David. *The Condition of Postmodernity: An Enquiry into the Origins of Cultural Change.* Oxford: Blackwell, 1989

Hussain, S. Abid: *The National Culture of India*, National Book Trust, New Delhi, 1956

Irigaray, Luce. *Speculum of the Other Woman.* Ithaca: Cornell University Press, 1985.

Iyengar, K.R. Srinivasa *Indian Writing in English*, Sterling, Delhi.

_____. "A Note on Anita Desai's Novels." *Banasthali Patrika*, 4 (January 1969), pp. 64-69.

Jain, Jasbir. *Stairs to the Attic: The Novels of Anita Desai.* Jaipur: Printwell, 1987.

_____. "Anita Desai." *Indian English Novelists* ed., Madhusudan Prasad. New Delhi: Sterling, 1982, pp. 23-50.

_____. "Anita Desai: Interviewed," *Rajasthan University Studies in English*, 12 (1979), 61-69.

_____. "The Changing Image of Gandhi in Indo-English Fiction," *Indian Literature*, XXII, 4, July-August 1979.

_____. "The Use of Fantasy in Anita Desai's Novels," *Explorations in Modern Indo-English Fiction,* ed. R.K. Dhawan. New Delhi: Bahri, 1982, pp. 227-37

Jain, Devaki, ed. *The Indian Woman.* New Delhi: Publications Division, 1973.

James, Henry, *The Art of the Novel: Critical Prefaces*. With an Introduction by Richard P. Blackmur. New York: Scribner, 1962

Jameson, Fredric. *The Political Unconscious: Narrative as a Socially Symbolic Act*, Ithaca, NY: Cornell University Press, 1981.

Jamkhandi, Sudhakar Ratnakar. "Artistic Effects of the Shifts in Point of View in Anita Desai's *Cry, the Peacock*." *Journal of Indian Writing in English*, Vol. IX, No. 1, Jan. 81, pp. 35-46.

Jardine, Alice. 'In the name of the modern: feminist questions d'après gynesis' in S. Sheridan, ed., *Grafts*, London: Verso, 1988, 15.

Jussawalla, Feroza and Reedway Dessenbrook, ed. *Interviews with Writers of the Postcolonial*. Press of Mississippi, 1992

Kanwar, Asha. *The Novels of Virginia Woolf and Anita Desai: A Comparative Study*. New Delhi: Prestige, 1989.

Kirpal, Vinay, Ed. *The New Indian Novel in English: A Study of the 1980*. New Delhi, Allied, 1990.

Kohli, Suresh. "Indian Women Novelists in English." *Times Weekly*, Nov. 1970, p. 3.

Krishna, Rao, A.V. *The Indo-Anglian Novel and the Changing Tradition: A Study of the Novels of Mulk Raj Anand, Kamala Markandaya, R.K. Narayan, and Raja Rao, 1930-1964*. Mysore: Rao and Raghavan, 1972.

_____. "Voices in the City, A Study," *Perspectives on Anita Desai*, ed. Ramesh K. Srivastava. Ghaziabad: Vimal, 1984.

Krishnaswamy, Shanta. *The Women in Indian Fiction in English*, Ashish, New Delhi, 1984, p. 213

Kumar, Shiv K. "The Fiction of Anita Desai: Another View." *The Humanities Review*, 3, July-December 1981, pp. 43-46.

Lal, P. Review of *Voices in the City*. *Littcrit*, Vol. 2, No. 2, Dec. 1976, pp. 51-53.

Lawrence, D.H. "Morality and Novel," Lodge, ed. *20th Century Literary Criticism*, 130.

Lewis, R.W.B. ed., *Herman Melville*, Dell., New York, 1962.

Lodge, David, ed. *Modern Criticism and Theory: A Reader*, London and New York: Longman, 1988.

Lyotard, Jean Francois. *The Postmodern Condition,* trans. G. Bennington and B. Mussumi. Minneapolis: University of Minnesota Press, 1984.

_____. *"Answering the question: what is postmodernism*? Trans. Regis Durand, in Lyotard.

_____. *Toward the Postmodern*, ed. Robert Harvey and Mark S. Roberts. Atlantic Highlands, NJ: Humanities Press, 1993.

_____. *The Postmodern Explained: Correspondence, 1982-1985*, trans. Don Barry, ed. Julian Pefanis and Morgan Thomas, Minneapolis: University of Minnesota Press, 1993.

Madhusudan, Prasad. *Anita Desai: The Novelist*. Allahabad: New Horizon, 1981.

Maini, Darshan Singh, *"Cry, the Peacock* as a Poetic Novel." *Indian Literature of the Past Fifty Years*, 1917-67, ed. C.D. Narasimhaiah Mysore: Mysore University, 1970, pp. 225-34.

_____. "The Achievement of Anita Desai" in K.K. Sharma, ed. *Indo-English Literature: A Collection of Critical Essays*. Ghaziabad: Vimal, 1977, pp. 215-30.

McHale, Brain. *Postmodernist Fiction*. London and New York: Methuen in Linda Hutcheon's *The Politics of Postmodernism*.

Mehta, Rama. *The Western Educated Hindu Women*. Bombay: Asia, 1970.

Morris, M. *Things To do With Shopping Centre* in S. Sheridan, ed. *Grafts*, London: Verso, 1988, 4.

Mukherjee Meenakshi, *Status of Women in India. A Synopsis of the Report of the National Committee* (New Delhi: Indian Council of Social Science Research, 1975), p. 29. Rep. in *The Twice Born Fiction* (New Delhi: Arnold-Heinemann, 1971).

_____ "Literature of Exile." *ACLALS Bulletin*, 4 (1974), pp. 27-32.

_____. "The Theme of Displacement in Anita Desai and Kamala Markandaya." *World Literature Written in English*, XVII, I (April, 1978), pp. 225-35.

Naik, M.K. et al. *Critical Essays on Indian Writing in English*. Karnataka University, Dharwar, 1968.

Naipaul, V.S. *India: A Wounded Civilization*. London: Penguin, 1979.

Narasimhaiah, C.D. *Moving Frontiers of English Studies in India*. S. Chand, New Delhi.

_____, ed. *Indian Literature of the Past Fifty Years (1917-1967)*. My sore: University of Mysore, 1970.

_____, ed. *Awakened Conscience: Studies in Commonwealth Literature*. New Delhi, Sterling, 1978.

Owens, Craig. "The Discourse of Others: Feminists and Postmodernism" in H. Foster, ed. *The Anti-Aesthetic: Essay on Postmodern Culture*. Port Townsend: Bay Press, 1983.

Pande, Mrinal. "Women without Men." Review of *Fire on the Mountain. The Times of India*, 18 Dec. 1977, p. 1.

Parameswaran, Uma. *A Study of Representative Indo-English Novelists.* New Delhi: Vikas, 1974.

Patel, Krishna Ahooja. "Another Development for Women" in *Approaches and Strategies*, ed. Marc Nerfin. Uppsala the Dag Hammarskjöld Foundation, 1977, 70.

Paul, Premila and R. Padmanabhan Nair, "Varieties of Loneliness in *Fire on the Mountain*," in *Indian Women Novelists*, R.K. Dhawan ed. New Delhi: Prestige, 1991, set I, Vol. III, pp. 216-35.

Poovya, Nimmie. "The Emergence of the Feminist Consciousness in Margaret Atwood's *Surfacing* and Anita Desai's *Where Shall We Go This Summer?" Commonwealth Literature: Problems of Response,* C.D. Narasimhaiah, ed. Madras. Macmillan, 1981, pp. 203-15.

Prasad, Amar Nath, ed. *Indian Women Novelists in English.* Atlantic, New Delhi, 2001.

Prasad, Hari Mohan. "Sound or Sense—A Study of Anita Desai's *Bye Bye, Blackbird." The Journal of Indian Writing in English*, IX, 1 (January 1981), 58-66.

Prasad, Madhusudan. *Anita Desai: The Novelist.* Allahabad: New Horizon, 1981, p. 54.

Rao, B. Ramachandra. *The Novels of Mrs. Anita Desai.* New Delhi: Kalyani, 1977.

_____. "Anita Desai: Themes and Variations in the Novels and Short Stories of Anita Desai." *Journal of Literature and Aesthetics*. II, 2-3 (April-July, 1982), 74-79.

Rao, Vimala. "Anita Desai's "*Where Shall We go This Summer?* An Analysis," *Commonwealth Quarterly*, 3-9 December 1978.

Raghavacharyulu, D.V.K., ed. *The Twofold Voice: Essays on Indian Writing in English* (1972)

Roy, M.N. Indian Renaissance Movement: Three Lecturers (1944) in *Indian Writing in English* by K.R. Srinivasa Iyengar, Sterling, New Delhi, 2002.

Sastry, Krishna L.S.R. "East-West Encounter in Indo-Anglican Fiction" *Essays and Studies*, ed. G.V.L.N. Sarma, Machilipatnam: Triveni, 1977, pp. 102-13.

Sethi, Sunil "Pieces of the Past," Review of Anita Desai's *Clear Light of Day, India Today,* December 1-15, 1980, p. 142.

Sharma, D.R. "Anita Desai." *The Tribune*, 2 April 1978.

Schorer, Mark. "Technique or Discovery," Handy and West, ed., *Twentieth Century Criticism: The Major Statements*, New Delhi, Light and Life Publication, 1976, pp.71-72.

Shanmugam, T.E. *Abnormal Psychology* (New Delhi: Tata McGraw Hill, 1981), p. 115.

Sharma, Atma Ram. *Essays on Indian-English Literature.* Aurangabad: Parimal, 1984.

_____. "An Interview with Anita Desai," *World Literature Written in English*, 16, No.1 (November 1971), 95-104. Reprinted in *Interviews with Indian-English Writers*, ed. Atma Ram, Calcutta: Writers Workshop, 1983, pp. 21-34.

Sharma, R.S. *Anita Desai.* New Delhi: Arnold Heinemann, 1981.

Sharma, Som P. and Kamal Awaste, "Anita Desai's *Cry, the Peacock*, A Vindication of the Feminine," in Ramesh K. Srivastava.

Sheth, Ketaki. "It's Fatal to Write an Audience in Mind." An Interview, *Imprint* (June, 1984).

Singh, Brijraj. *"The Fiction of Anita Desai." The Humanities Review* III, 2, July-December, 1981.

Sivaramakishna H. "From Alienation to Mythic Acceptance: The Ordeal of Consciousness in Anita Desai's Fiction." *Kakatiya Journal of English Studies.* 1 (1978), pp. 7-26.

Srivastava, Ramesh K. *Perspectives on Anita Desai*, Vimal, Ghaziabad, 1984

_____. "Anita Desai at Work: An Interview," in *Perspectives on Anita Desai.* Ghaziabad: Vimal, 1984, pp. 208-27.

Thomas, O.J. "The Enslaved and the Unsolved: The Characters of Anand and Anita Desai," *Quest*, Vol. 12, June, 1998.

Vijay Kumar, T. *"Review of in Custody," Indian Book Chronicle,* X 17-18, Sept 1-10, pp. 286-87.

Vinson, James. Anita Desai's Comments in *Contemporary Novelists*, ed. New York: St. Martin's Press, 1972, p. 348.

Walker, Barbara G. *The Crone, Woman of Age, Wisdom and Power.* New York: Harper, 1985, p. 59.

Walter, Allen. *The English Novel*, London: Penguin, 1954, p. 303.

Wolff, J. "Feminine Sentences: Essays on Women and Culture," *A Readers Guide to Contemporary Feminist Literary Criticism*, Cambridge: Polity Press, 1990, 160.